BOY VEY!

Also by Kristina Grish

We Need to Talk. But First, Do You Like My Shoes?:
Dress Codes for Dumping Your Man

BOY VEY!

*The
Shiksa's Guide
to Dating
Jewish Men*

By Kristina Grish
Illustrated by LULU*

SIMON SPOTLIGHT ENTERTAINMENT

New York   London   Toronto   Sydney

To my mother, who always says that if she could do it
over, she'd marry a Jewish man (Sorry, Dad.)

SSE

SIMON SPOTLIGHT ENTERTAINMENT
An imprint of Simon & Schuster
1230 Avenue of the Americas, New York, New York 10020
Text copyright © 2005 by Kristina Grish
Illustrations copyright © 2005 by LULU*
SIMON SPOTLIGHT ENTERTAINMENT and related logo are
trademarks of Simon & Schuster, Inc.
Designed by Yaffa Jaskoll
The text of this book was set in Bembo.
Manufactured in the United States of America
First Edition 10 9 8 7 6 5 4 3 2 1
Library of Congress Cataloging-in-Publication Data
Grish, Kristina.
Boy vey! : the Shiksa's guide to dating Jewish men /
by Kristina Grish.— 1st ed.
p. cm.
ISBN 0-689-87889-3
1. Interfaith dating. 2. Mate selection. 3. Man-woman relationships.
4. Jewish men—Psychology. 5. Single women—Social life and customs.
I. Title.
HQ801.8.G75 2005
646.7'7—dc22
2004026686

CONTENTS

FOREWORD

About a Girl

Midway through dinner on Christmas Eve, my mother and I scraped brisket fat into the trash can. "I just love this Kristina," my mom gushed, conspiratorially sharing a questionable hunk of sweet meat. "She eats, she cooks, she's funny, she's warm, she's a beautiful girl, and she has a great job. Did you notice how she served you my potatoes without even asking?" Mom put the plates in the sink and looked me seriously in the eye. "Benjamin," my mother solemnly said, this after Kristina had promised her a discount on shoes through her magazine connections, "I think she's a great multitasker—and you know how important that is to running a household." Kristina and I were home for the holidays—which meant Hanukkah for me, Christmas for her—and before the Costco pie had even been sliced, Mom had given Kristina her ultimate blessing: She was family material.

This Shiksa could clearly do Jew.

When I first met Kristina, I thought she was Jewish. Dressed impeccably in a crisp white blouse beneath razor-thin black leather, she let me in on the complexities of her fast-paced life before I even said eight words. She told me about her colorful family, her publishing job, her dating history—and the next three vertical moves *I* should make to advance my hemorrhaging career.

I finally piped up. "I think the restaurant is on Twenty-third Street."

"Oh, do you mean El Quijote?" she asked. "We can't eat there. I know a much better, out-of-the-way Honduran chorizo spot in the West Village." Kristina swept me into an idling yellow cab.

"Where did you go to Hebrew school?" I asked.

"I'm not Jewish," she whispered coyly, and then: "I'm a Shiksa."

That night was the start of a unique relationship, which opened my eyes to the similarities between faiths. It seems that all women—Christian, Jew, or otherwise— were put on this earth to bust chops. But to find a Shiksa with a hilariously high-maintenance mixture of strength and prowess is an utter utopia for the libidinous Jew. We can rebel against our history, while having great sex too. To the nebbish young Heeb who prowls the city at dusk on the Sabbath, Kristina—and her Shiksa cohorts—

represents the best of both worlds: familiar yet exotic, proper yet fun, sweet yet stern, comforting yet challenging.

Kristina and I spent the better part of the next two years together. That is, before she left me for my coworker (Jewish), then roommate (Jewish), then roommate's younger brother (who, of course, is also a Jew). Who better to write the book on interfaith coupling? Kristina knows why racquetball triumphs over squash, where to find the best steam baths in Manhattan, and how summer camp turns Jewish boys into men. Speaking as an ex and a Jew, I dually approve the lessons in *Boy Vey!*—and guarantee they'll wow even the toughest moms over brisket.

—Ben Kaplan

ACKNOWLEDGMENTS

I'd like to thank everyone who doled out some serious mitzvahs as I wrote this book. I have the deepest appreciation for my very favorite go-to Jews: Amy Hersh, Ben Kaplan, Andrew Kessler, Maggie Nemser, and Johnny Vulkan. And to the sexiest Shiksas I know—Allison Keane, Erin Lynch, Alva Polinsky, Alia Malley, Laura Paterson, and Margaux Caniato—for their endless patience, humor, and interest in a project I suspect they never fully understood. To Scott Mebus, who will always make me laugh and believe in past lives (please admit you were Jewish, already). To Mom, who taught me to explore men's differences, and to Dad, for never judging my erratic taste. Gena Grish, you're an emotional whiz at twenty-three. To Ryan Fischer-Harbage, my dedicated editor, and Elisabeth Weed, my faithful and fabulous agent. And to all the Jewish men in my world, who've encouraged me to embrace your beautiful culture: Thank you for your love and your lessons—but I could have done without the smelly fish.

Oh, admit it: At some point in your adult life, you've wanted to snag a Hebrew honey. Or maybe you already have. Or maybe you're snuggled next to him right now, reading this sentence and wishing you'd thought of this book idea before I did.

In any case, who can blame you? There's a lot to love about a guy who makes your laughter his priority, who talks about your relationship more than you do, who's wildly intense inside the bedroom and out, who thinks nudging him up the corporate ladder is a sign of affection. Jewish men feed your mind and appetite, and they are the ultimate caretakers without a hint of machismo. They're also generous and thoughtful, thanks to a matriarchal culture that's taught them to appreciate women's strength, candor, humor, and intelligence. And because Jewish men value professional drive, your mom can finally tell neighbors that you're dating a doctor, lawyer, or entrepreneur. And she'll mean it this time.

Of course, dating a nice Jewish boy comes with its caveats—most obvious, the whole Messiah thing. The good news is that if you're dating a Jew, he's likely either Reform or simply acculturated, and thus, open-minded about mixing it up a bit. (Unless conversion is your idea of a hot first-date topic, don't waste your time with Conservative and Orthodox observances.) Whether your love mensch is super religious is seldom the issue. I've found that interfaith coupling gets most sticky—and believe me, this Presbyterian has dated enough Jews to make their ancestors shvitz in their graves—when wondering how to navigate daily interactions: how to deal with his obsessive hand-wringing, what to expect from his sex drive, how to survive his mom's verbal hemophilia. Interfaith relationship snafus arise because Jewish cultural nuances are ingrained in his psyche and not in yours. So if you want to hang with a Jew, you need to identify with his faith and lifestyle.

So what's a Shiksa? Well, you. The word is simply Yiddish for a non-Jewish woman, though the term carries a long history of cultural weight that's far too academic and arguable for the attention span of dating-guide devotees (myself included). Suffice it to say that Shiksas are traditionally viewed as the attractive, mysterious, and forbidden other—and not always in a flattering way. However, most of the young, Jewish studs I meet insist that the femme fatale rep is an antiquated ideal that's upheld more by their older parents and grandparents than by today's cooler Bens, Joshes, and Andrews. Thank heaven! When it comes to compatibility issues, your religion (or lack thereof) is but one part of your gorgeous profile—and ranks right up there with charisma, looks, education, family, ethnicity, and bra size. Honestly, your cutie doesn't adore you because he wants to explore your hidden temptress or piss off his family. And if you suspect he does, dump the loser and hide his yarmulke. Because you, my dear, can do better.

Since you bought this book, I'm going to assume you have an elementary knowledge of the Jewish faith and its lingo (or at least a piqued interest). Beyond apologies for your beliefs or stereotypes about his, here's what you won't find in these pages: basic Judaic principles, long history lessons, Hebrew prayer translations, funeral downers, extreme holiday traditions like Purim or Simchas Torah, or three cheers for interfaith marriage. *Boy Vey!: The Shiksa's Guide to Dating Jewish Men* is simply that—a fun dating guide written for outsiders, by an outsider. Not to mention, one who's proved to be a natural at the Jewish dating shtick (or so the exes and mothers say) . . . and sees no reason why you can't be too!

Who's Who in Every Jewish Man's Heart

To land an interested Jew, it helps to know the icons that color his worldview. According to one of my exes, Ben, a journalist now living in Toronto with his Greek Orthodox girlfriend, you're bound to impress by memorizing a few Jewish star-studded majors. Since circumcision, Ben's only dated non-Jews—and fancies himself "something of an expert at getting crossover chicks up to speed about members of the tribe. This includes celebrity hitters that make up our common soul." Here, Ben's reckless intro into what he claims is the carefully narrow, frighteningly like-minded Jewish male POV.

The Reason Your Boyfriend Chases Shiksas Like You:
Tori Spelling

The Interfaith Duo He Admires Most:
Ben Stiller and Christine Taylor

Who He Thinks Would Play Him in a Movie:
Jake Gyllenhaal

More Likely, Even on a Good Day:
David Schwimmer

The Jewish Comedian He Thinks He Channels:
Jon Stewart

The Jewish Comedian He Really Channels:
Larry David

His Jewish Fight Song:

Adam Sandler's "Chanukah Song"

His Jewish Bible:

Portnoy's Complaint by Philip Roth

His Jewish God:

Woody Allen, circa *Manhattan*

His Jewish Colin Powell:

Madeleine Albright

The Only Jew Cool Enough to Be Friends with Jack Kerouac:

Allen Ginsberg

Another Cool Jew:

Lenny Bruce

An Off-Again, On-Again Cool Jew Who's Kind of Like Lenny Bruce:

Howard Stern

The Lapsed Catholic He Thinks Is Turning Judaism into Scientology:

Madonna

Her Jewish Friend Who Can Do No Wrong:
Gwyneth Paltrow

The Jew All Jews Wish They Could Give Back:
David Berkowitz, Son of Sam

"Did You Hear About . . . ?"

Joanna, a Methodist editor from Michigan, grew up in an über-WASP town but was always drawn to Jewish men. "I casually dated' a Jewish guy sophomore year, then another for a year and a half. I'm approaching a year with my most recent Jewish boyfriend," she recounts. "I guess you could call that a type." A type that Joanna says is "passionate and really deep"—especially when it comes to analyzing identity, religion, life, and death. "My Catholic and Protestant exes were into acting really chill and cool, but never funny or philosophical," she says. Although someone who's never experienced Joanna's dating life might consider this stereotyping, she insists her Jewish boyfriends can dish it *and* take it. "When I dated my first serious boyfriend, he made me watch *Annie Hall* with him. He joked that he was Woody Allen, and that I was Annie—which annoyed me a little, because Annie's kind of a bitch." Sounds like Joanna's not the only one who typecasts. . . .

Shadchen, Shadchen, Make Me a Shiddach

Barbie Adler is president and CEO of Selective Search Inc., the nation's leading upscale matchmaking firm. Barbie, raised on the North Shore of Chicago, is also an authentic Shadchen (Yiddish for "matchmaker") who's shared relationship advice with *Fortune, Forbes, Oprah,* and *CNN Headline News*. Since pairing happy duos is Barbie's biz, she's created eight Jewish bachelor/Shiksa profiles for us. How much do *you* really know about interfaith compatibility? Make your matches, then compare to Barbie's picks!

Meet the Dating Pool

Bachelor One: Jeffrey

Age: 31
Job Title: Vice President, Investments
Hometown: New York, New York
Likes: Heady family dinners at the club, *New York Times* op-ed columns
Best Qualities: Exceptional golfer, avid reader, knows Thomas Pink sales staff by name
Last Relationship: Met last girlfriend at the "Break the Fast" dance at the Waldorf Astoria
Profile: Works in mergers and acquisitions. Confident, sarcastic, tidy. Bought brownstone to rent out on recommendation of Mom, a real estate broker.

Bachelor Two: Avi

Age: 24
Job Title: Internet Producer by day, Party Promoter by night
Hometown: San Francisco, California
Likes: Obsessively checking his BlackBerry, VIP rooms, and velvet ropes

Best Qualities: Hot, charming, connected

Last Relationship: Six months of office sex with his assistant art director

Profile: Son of a catering mogul, but plans to franchise when he inherits the business. He loves all things new, fast, and highly interactive (women and technology). Likes to be "in the know," so he subscribes to *Forbes* and *Us Weekly*.

Bachelor Three: Adrien

Age: 28

Job Title: TV Editor turned Stand-up Comic

Hometown: Princeton, New Jersey

Likes: Karaoke, skiing, vending machine snacks

Best Qualities: Silliness, adventurous spirit, no edit button

Last Relationship: Two weeks with a Minneapolis figure skater

Profile: Performs at bar mitzvahs, hospitals, and funerals. Peers at film school and news stations giggled at him, not with him. Misunderstood Adrien now chases his funny bone full time. He'd also be happy playing Mr. Mom before age thirty.

Shiksa Four: **Megan**

Age: 24

Job Title: Veterinarian

Hometown: Tucson, Arizona

Likes: Trips to the herbalist, adopting cows from veal farms, dreadlocks on stoner boys

Longest relationship: Five years with her brother's best friend

Profile: Works at a small hospital, but put herself through vet school as a day care nanny on an Alaskan cruise line. Ideal date is dinner and the aquarium. Wants 2.5 kids and a picket fence—made of hemp.

Meet the Happy Couples

Jeffrey and Katie

Barbie Says: Jeffrey's WASP-y Jew style lends itself to Katie's J.Crew fantasies. She's great eye candy for his business dinners. Will have more throw pillows than sex on an overpriced antique bed.

Avi and Tiffany

Barbie Says: They'll have a nice life . . . on Page Six. As a publicist and Daddy's little girl, Tiffany knows how to be entertaining and opportunistic. Avi appreciates her upkeep: career, smooth skin, and Beamer.

Jacob and Julie

Barbie Says: He's upwardly mobile; she's happily grounded. Julie's student stories are a refreshing sub for family dinner debates. Especially when in-laws want grandkids, pronto.

Adrien and Megan

Barbie Says: Stand-up comedy isn't easy, even if your people have years of irony under their Borscht Belt. Adrien needs a nurturer like Megan to quell insecurities and bolster self-confidence. Curious and accepting, he'll support her PETA passions. Karaoke skills will entertain kids.

CHAPTER 2

You Probably Won't Meet
Him in Wyoming . . .

It's no secret you're dying to run your fingers through the curly locks of your own Mr. Tall, Dark, and Circumcised. So where are these candidly chatty, extremely bright, terribly passionate, neurotically driven, self-deprecatingly funny, and obsessively self-aware men to be found?

Everywhere. Strategically speaking of course.

Although Jewish population demographics are expectedly on your side in states like New York, California, Florida, Illinois, and New Jersey, you shouldn't just throw in the his-and-her towels if you live in South Dakota or the Bible Belt (Palm Beach is just a quick jaunt away . . .). In fact, you may have a better chance of meeting a Jewish babe in an area that has fewer Jews total, but where Jewish people constitute a higher percentage of the state's total head count—like in DC and Massachusetts. Population density works to your favor, and the numbers game, in which he's an overall minority, may also make your looks and background less outstanding. I've included a state-by-state breakdown of population odds, thanks to the U.S. Census Bureau, in the pretty chart below. You do the math, my aspiring Mrs. Einstein.

Where There's Not Too Few a Jew

	Estimated Jewish Population	Total Population*	Jewish Percent of Total
Alabama	9,000	4,451,000	0.2
Alaska	3,400	628,000	0.5
Arizona	81,500	5,165,000	1.6
Arkansas	1,700	2,678,000	0.1
California	999,000	34,000,000	2.9
Colorado	73,000	4,323,000	1.7
Connecticut	111,000	3,410,000	3.2
Delaware	13,500	786,000	1.7
District of Columbia	25,500	571,000	4.5
Florida	620,000	16,054,000	3.9

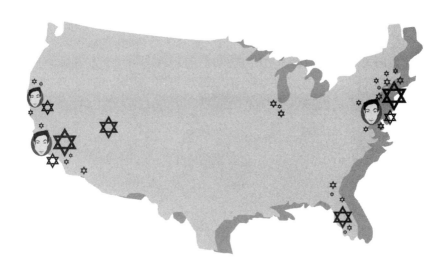

	Estimated Jewish Population	Total Population*	Jewish Percent of Total
Georgia	93,500	8,230,000	1.1
Hawaii	7,000	1,212,000	0.6
Idaho	1,100	1,299,000	0.1
Illinois	270,000	12,436,000	2.2
Indiana	17,500	6,090,000	0.3
Iowa	6,100	2,928,000	0.2
Kansas	14,000	2,692,000	0.5
Kentucky	11,500	4,047,000	0.3
Louisiana	16,000	4,470,000	0.4
Maine	9,300	1,277,000	0.7
Maryland	213,000	5,311,000	4.0
Massachusetts	275,000	6,357,000	4.3
Michigan	110,000	9,952,000	1.1
Minnesota	42,000	4,931,000	0.9

	Estimated Jewish Population	Total Population★	Jewish Percent of Total
Mississippi	1,500	2,849,000	0.1
Missouri	62,500	5,603,000	1.1
Montana	800	903,000	0.1
Nebraska	7,000	1,713,000	0.4
Nevada	77,000	2,019,000	3.8
New Hampshire	10,000	1,240,000	0.8
New Jersey	485,000	8,429,000	5.7
New Mexico	11,500	1,821,000	0.6
New York	1,657,000	18,990,000	8.7
North Carolina	26,500	8,077,000	0.3
North Dakota	450	641,000	0.1
Ohio	149,000	11,360,000	1.3
Oklahoma	5,000	3,453,000	0.1
Oregon	32,000	3,429,000	0.9
Pennsylvania	282,000	12,283,000	2.3
Rhode Island	16,000	1,050,000	1.5
South Carolina	11,500	4,023,000	0.3
South Dakota	300	756,000	(z)
Tennessee	18,000	5,702,000	0.3
Texas	131,000	20,947,000	0.6
Utah	4,500	2,242,000	0.2
Vermont	5,500	610,000	0.9
Virginia	66,000	7,104,000	0.9
Washington	43,000	5,908,000	0.7

	Estimated Jewish Population	Total Population*	Jewish Percent of Total
West Virginia	2,300	1,808,000	0.1
Wisconsin	28,000	5,372,000	0.5
Wyoming	400	494,000	0.1
Total	**6,155,000	282,125,000	2.2

Totals may not be exact due to rounding.

*Resident population, April 1, 2001 (Source: U.S. Bureau of the Census).

**Exclusive of Puerto Rico and the Virgin Islands, which previously reported Jewish populations of 1,500 and 350, respectively.

(z) Figure is less than 0.1 and rounds to 0.

Source: David Singer, Ed. *American Jewish Year Book 2002,* NY: American Jewish Committee, 2002.

If You Don't Have the Patience to Skim Government Charts . . .

. . . then you'll need to rely on clever wiles to find yourself a charming Jewish man. Forget online dating sites or family introductions—especially when it's much more fun to intuitively sniff out his Gucci cologne. The secret? Consider your target's recreational interests, educational priorities, professional goals, and familial obligations. This is hardly the time to "meet him when you least expect it." (What does that *mean,* anyway?)

To start, look for events hosted by men whose first names include Adam, Josh, David, Noah, or Sam—and last names end with "-schwartz," "-hersh," "-witz," "-berg," or "-stein." If you don't bed the MC, you probably have a shot with friends he's invited to watch him moderate. Even the most melancholy events are opportunities to meet a cute Jew. If you're a shrewd Shiksa, a morose funeral in Great Neck, New York, could suddenly turn into a blessing from above.

That's why I've listed a few cunning spots where you're bound to locate the studs of your interfaith dreams (these aren't state-specific). Some settings are more obvious than others, but all promise overwhelming prospects if you play your gin rummy cards right.

Comedy Clubs:

Either onstage or chortling through a two-drink minimum

A Florida Beach Condo:

Jews don't summer, they winter. Martha's Vineyard, Cape Cod, East Hampton, Hilton Head, Nantucket, and Myrtle Beach are for men who wear gingham and replace first names with surnames like Preston II and Coleman IV (more than once, no less).

The Coldest Subway Car:

Relishing the cheap, air-conditioned ride on a muggy day

Small-Business Line at the Bank:

Mentally calculating his tax write-offs

Napping:

Anywhere with back support

Annual Mother's Day Sale at Macy's:

Buying crystal tsatskes at 50 percent off—then asking for an additional 10 percent because the sea lion's flipper is chipped

Basketball Courts:

Playing shirts versus skins with his buddies and their man boobs, or eating Kosher dogs while sitting front row at the play-offs (and suffering from six-pack envy)

Deli:

Buying a pastry, ordering lean pastrami, or chomping on a pickle

Reading:

Think books by Philip Roth, Saul Bellow, Larry King

A Madonna Concert:

Praying the Kabbalah convert will sing "Like a Virgin" in Yiddish

Rhinoplasty Waiting Room:

Pretending to meet his sister after her consultation

Chinese Restaurant:

On Sundays

Chinese Restaurant and Movie Theater:

On Christmas Day

Concerts:

Flicking his Bic to Bob Dylan, Simon and Garfunkel, and Neil Diamond. If we're talking hip-hop, he's probably a backer.

Prescription Counter at the Drugstore:

Buying generic

Lobbies of Investment Banks:

Obsessing over plunging stocks and fanaticizing about plunging necklines

Nell Carter's Grave:

Gimme a break! You didn't know she was Jewish?

University Library:

Studying diligently. Feel free to mentally create a Dating Dewey Decimal, since the good ones sit together by interest and professional goals.

Real Estate Open House:

Estimating how much his own space is worth, relatively speaking

Tennis Camp:

Wondering if he has to tip the ball boy

NYC's Diamond District:

Haggling for his little sister's Sweet Sixteen

An Airport Boarding Gate to Illinois:

Hopping a plane to a family reunion in Highland Park

In the Produce Aisle:

Shopping as an elderly escort and DOROT volunteer

Tasti D-Lite Shop:

Debating between peanut butter and rice pudding ice cream substitutes. Certified Kosher and 99 percent fat free! Yum.

Jewish Community Center (JCC) Events:

Hoarding Purell on group camping trips or running the grill on singles night barbeques. Sure, you'll stand out as the token Shiksa. But isn't that the point?

Jerusalem:

Or so I've heard.

If You're in the Mood to Schmooze . . .

Should you suddenly wish to visit an old college room-mate or long-lost auntie, you may as well time your trip with annual conventions that teem with Jewish professionals. Mark the most convenient months in your planner, but call each organization to confirm locations and hotel arrangements. What's not to love about New Orleans in August?

American Psychiatric Association

Often in May, MDs gather in big cities such as Atlanta and New York. In October, the Institute on Psychiatric Services meets annually in Atlanta. How does that make you feel?

American Psychological Association

If your idea of dating perks doesn't include free Prozac, meet a cute shrink between late July and late August.

Sites change every year, but past cities included DC, Boston, Chicago, San Francisco, New Orleans, and even Hawaii. Aloha, analysis!

American Medical Association

Ever so reliable, the best docs annually convene mid-June in Chicago. Is that your heart beating or mine?

American Institute of Certified Public Accountants

Spring meetings hit in April or May in locales including DC and Arizona. Come autumn, number crunchers crowd convention halls in New Orleans and Orlando. Specific workshops are also held in sunny spots like California and Puerto Rico. Just think: If you snag a CPA, someone else can try to balance your checkbook.

National Bar Association

Lawyers may meet until the wee hours, but once lectures and debates finish, you're in for some bona fide fun. Close the case on your love life in late July or early August—in cities like Orlando, San Francisco, Dallas, Charlotte, and New Orleans.

CHAPTER 3

Summer Camp Is Not a Cult
(and Other Honest Mistakes)

Growing up male lends itself to certain rites of passage from which you, as a female and your guy's new hottie, are obviously excluded: his first beer, first kiss, first girl-friend, first lay, first lay with a virgin, first lay with a slut who says she's a virgin . . . You get the point. Add to this issue the fact that most of your guy's manly education occurred within religious structures—even if his family encourages it more for cultural reasons than godly ones—and I'd be shocked if you *weren't* curious about what's happened to him behind closed doors.

Jewish or not, you've spent enough time with exes and your therapist to realize that to understand any adult, you must first appreciate his upbringing. The difference here is that unlike your ex-goyfriend who still talks about his first high school touchdown, your current man will never stop yapping about Jewish milestones like Hebrew school, his bar mitzvah, summer camp, Teen Tour, youth group, and his Jewish fraternity. Your sweetie claims to be all grown up—but after you listen to a twenty-minute story about how he led a midnight raid on the girls' cabin at Camp Comet, I agree it's highly debatable.

My advice? Once the reminiscing begins, don't avoid the fish tales—especially if he's with Jewish friends who join in. As his interested Shiksa, listen carefully and laugh politely. Even if the stories suck, they'll yield insight into his identity, values, and dating history. Should his enthusiastic rambling hit a nerve, change the subject to female rites of passage such as your first mani/pedi or yeast infection. He'll take the hint.

Rather than relive *every* milestone, I'll simply detail the three landmark events he'll revisit most with friends and family. You need only a primer—because believe me, he'll fill in the rest.

And You Thought Getting Your Period Was a Big Deal?

When your boyfriend was a pimply young Jew, years of Hebrew school and months of bar mitzvah prep ended with a stressful read from the Torah (the book that dictates Judaic principles and customs) on a Saturday morning near his thirteenth birthday. After chanting in Hebrew with a crackling voice, he partied like a rock star at a celebration thrown in his honor. He called himself bar mitzvah boy.

Although modest luncheons aren't unusual, most Jewish parents throw down crazy cash—up to $30,000—to usher their son into bar mitzvah-ed manhood. Family, friends, classmates, and business associates give checks, stocks, and gifts to the newly inducted while a pushy band or DJ insists awkward teens dance and play games. Need a visual? Tall girls with short boys, and swollen toes and even more swollen erections. Balloons galore.

While you were busy fantasizing about debutante balls and asking Mom if you could borrow her maxis with wings, your boyfriend had a packed social calendar of parties featuring over-the-top decorations, entertainment, and souvenirs at an event where adults often ate better than kids (seared tuna versus fried chicken). Although sports, rock bands, movies, and magic were common party themes, I've been told that more creative efforts included "Phantom of the Opera," "Fiesta!," "Haunted House," "The Love Boat," and "Beverly Hills 90210" (hello, only Andrea was Jewish?). If your boyfriend's party had a theme such as "Sunday in the

Park . . . with Sam," at which guests dressed like characters in the Georges Seurat painting, you're in for one high-maintenance courtship.

"My bar mitzvah theme was 'Extreme Sports.' It was when BMX bikes and skateboarding were really cool," says Brad, a car dealer in Los Angeles. "We gave out T-shirts that said, 'It was rad at Brad's bar mitzvah.'" Wish I were there! Leaving with loot like Brad's shirts or a custom-made chocolate bar is always a bar mitzvah highlight. This is second only to Kodak moments with chopped liver and ice sculptures carved in the honoree's likeness.

Who Likes Spaghetti Night This Much?

Growing up, I had a few friends whose parents shipped them to Girl Scout or talent camps—as long as they didn't interrupt summer vacations to Disneyland or Pennsylvania Dutch Country. Religious camps were for zealots, and any other rustic getaway was simply an excuse to torture teens into submission with watered-down Kool-Aid, public humiliation via skits, and really cheap sheets.

Your Jewish boyfriend, however, tells a completely different story about beloved coed summer camp. "I went for the canoe trips, cabin raids, and overall camaraderie," says rad Brad, who did major time at Camp Scatico. "I went for twelve years straight, missing only one year in between." So at what age do they cut campers off? "They don't *cut people off*," he says, slightly miffed. "I know a male counselor who's in his forties. I only stopped going because I had to take an internship when I finished college. I'm trying to convince my wife to go back for a summer, with our child." Um, something tells me she'd probably prefer Canyon Ranch in the Berkshires.

As you might guess, Jewish camp's about more than roasting marshmallows over an open fire. It's also about igniting flames during the stretch of a boy's adolescent development—which means bunk life represents independence, friendship, and, of course, sex. Josh, a music producer from Northridge, California, who spent two meaningful years at Camp Shalom in Malibu Canyon, isn't the only guy I know who had his first kiss while smelling of bug spray. "I was considered one of the cute guys at camp, so the girls liked me and the guys respected me," says Josh modestly. "Sessions last three to four weeks, and most people stay for more than one session, so you create a lot of emotional connections. You sing songs with your arms around each other at the campfire. You dress up once a week and hang out with people from the same background. It's a very family-oriented environment. . . ." Cut the crap, Josh. Camp is about unsupervised access to chicks, and you know it. "Yeah, there was the girl thing," he laughs. "After curfew, we'd keep our clothes on, then sneak candy into the girls' bunks. The beach was right there. If I could relive any part of my life, it would be camp." Even Brad admits there's something to an open sky and shared outhouse that revs a couple's hormones. "Camp was a place to prove your manhood," he admits. "For me, it was a big deal when I was twenty-one and had sex with a counselor that was forty-three at the time." About wanting to head back to camp with your wife, Brad? When she reads this, your chances are kind of shot to hell.

Although some coed camps are more religious than others, even the most Reform feature Shabbat dinner on Friday (to honor the day God rested after creating the universe) and Saturday night observances. If your boyfriend was a die-hard camper, he probably started young and made it to CIT classes (that's Counselor in Training to you). Lorin—a Catholic Broadway dancer who married Howard, a Jewish summer camp devotee from the age of eight—has trouble swallowing the camp thing. "My parents used to joke that if I didn't behave, they'd send me to camp like Jewish parents. It was hard enough getting their permission to attend slumber parties. I can't imagine eight weeks in the woods with strangers!" she laughs. "But Howard can horseback ride and play tennis much better than I. He has camp friends and professionally networks with past campers. I envy that a little." Enough to let her kids follow Dad's lead? "I say no to camp, but Howard says yes. If I ever need a break, we'll see. But never before the age of thirteen." That's what they all say.

Teen Tours—and Your Boyfriend, the Ultimate Groupie

During your guy's formative years, he probably joined Jewish friends for the infamous Teen Tour: a guided trip to hot spots in the United States and Europe but most popularly Israel. Here, more than two hundred sweaty sophomores live in pseudo-dorms and on a kibbutz for a week (Hebrew for "communal settlement;" kind of like a Jewish commune). In Israel, kids travel every sandy nook and cranny of the Promised Land for two months as an unspoken religious duty. At this point in your man's maturation process, his attachment to his homeland is pretty strong.

Though again, and not to diminish the trip's religious impact, God knows Teen Tours aren't just about visiting the Dead Sea. "Israel was such an influential trip, educational in more ways than one," says Josh, our horny camper from Cali. "I smoked my first cigarette, snuck out and went to clubs, screwed around with hot Israeli girls. It was as much about becoming a man as it was about becoming a Jewish man. The tour was also very religious, and I learned a lot about the country's history." Taught by hot Israeli girls, I'm sure.

How to Tell a Man by His Yarmulke

Repeat after me: Yah-mah-ka. A yarmulke, or "kippah" in Hebrew, is the small, disklike skullcap your boyfriend wears to temple or during Shabbat dinner—and probably collects from past weddings. Why the beanie? Tradition says man shows respect to God by covering his head. Although your sweetheart could easily sport one of the free, black vinyl yarmulkes kept in a basket near the shul's (temple's) entrance, he probably has his own for sanitary or style reasons. You know you've already judged him by his Hush Puppies. Why should his bobby-pinned topper be off-limits?

The "Just Like Butta" Yarmulke:

Wearing leather or suede, he's a fashion-conscious high roller. Expect him to romance you in overpriced steak houses, but never in a car with fabric interior.

The "Rub My Head" Yarmulke:

Satin and velvet insist that he's smooth. Foil embossed yarmulke details—rainbow swirls, music notes, Stars of David, or the Jerusalem skyline—say he's flashy.

The "Somebody Has a Hobby" Yarmulke:

Always the spectator, he's proud of his athletic affiliations. Hand-painted baseballs, hockey pucks, tennis balls, and basketballs are for aspiring jocks. Team logos scream die-hard fan, while chess-piece stitch work whispers, "I'm quirky."

The "Just Plain Fun" Yarmulke:

Mr. Life of the Party couldn't be more of a show-off. He'll always toast the host in novelty kippahs with hearts, keyboards, bagels, computers, hot chilies, champagne glasses—and of course, matzo. Trendy? Not so much.

The "Always a Politician" Yarmulke:

He's as devoted to the Israeli flag design as he is to the American one. If your man sports a pro-Lieberman kippah, beware: He's the type that won't let go.

The "Look, I'm Circular Too" Yarmulke:

Watermelons, pool balls, Frisbees, flowers. If the object on the yarmulke mimics its circular shape, the kippah is a keeper. Similarly, your man will do everything to fit in and make you happy—and that's anything but square.

Play That Funky Music, White Boy . . .

Scott, a Catholic bar mitzvah DJ (yes, I just said that) from Harwich, Massachusetts, spins for hormonally charged teens during their bar mitzvah parties. Although he occasionally lets the guest of honor get his groove on to the Beastie Boys and top 40 hits, Scott focuses on Motown, disco, and oldies sets to really draw a crowd to the dance floor.

Why should you care? While dating a Jewish man, you'll probably be invited to the bar mitzvah of a friend or family member. You'll also be expected to dance, which helps you bond with his extended circle. Here, Scott shares his top ten playlist and rates each tune (out of five) by how important it will be to guests that you shake that moneymaker. And by moneymaker, I mean your rear . . . not the bar mitzvah boy.

"Celebration" by Kool and the Gang ★★★

"We Are Family" by Sister Sledge ★★★★

"The Chicken Dance" by Bob Kames and the
Happy Organ ★

"Electric Slide" by Grandmaster Slice ★★★

"Gonna Make You Sweat (Everybody Dance
Now)" by C&C Music Factory ★★★

"Hot Hot Hot" by Buster Poindexter ★★

"Respect" by Aretha Franklin ★★★★

"Wind Beneath My Wings" by Bette Midler ★★

"Summer Wind" by Frank Sinatra ★★★★

"Hava Nagila" traditional ★★★★★

"Did You Hear About . . . ?"

P.J., an attorney from Atlantic City, agreed to make the
requisite trip to Israel—but boarded the bus kicking and
screaming. "All I wanted to do was spend my summer at
the shore with non-Jewish friends," P.J. remembers.

During high school, P.J. says he rebelled against religious mandates, as his Jewish peers memorized their prayers. "I felt like such a small Jew, sometimes. During Hebrew school, everyone talked about the Palestinian uprising and this big trip to Israel," he says. "I just went to look at the girls—and then never date them. I dated one Jewish girl in my life, and she happened to have back hair. Never again . . ."

During week five of the six-week tour, kids' families were invited to visit—but because P.J. and his friend Eric complained so much about whining campers and scary bus bombs, P.J.'s father treated them to a room at the Hilton in Tel Aviv instead. The two took tennis and sailing lessons, and gorged themselves at a Russian restaurant. "We had a blast, but after a while we did what any little horny, playboy, clueless idiots with slicked-back hair and complimentary yellow robes would do," P.J. laughs. "We threw a party." He and Eric bought two cases of beer and invited fellow campers from the kibbutz to their room. Alas, the Hugh Hefnerstein twins lost their moxie when a camper snitched. P.J. and Eric were sent home. "I remember the leader scolding, 'I just want you to know that the rest of the week your friends will be hiking across forty-five miles of the Negev Desert in 106-degree heat . . . and you'll be going home!'" P.J.

says. "All I could think was, *'Hallelujah!'*" P.J. and Eric were stoked but scared of their fathers' wrath. But when P.J.'s dad greeted the duo at the airport, he promptly bought them a lavish dinner. He'd ordered P.J. and Eric home all right . . . but only to relieve them of their misery.

CHAPTER 4

Because Neurosis and Guilt Are Part of His DNA

Is it actually possible that your lover boy overanalyzes more than *you* do? Is it ever! Think about it: Sigmund Freud and Woody Allen—both of whom are celebrated for their psyches—are the two most prototypical figures in recent history of Jewish neurosis and guilt (let's call it N&G for short; kind of like S&M, except the whips and chains are mental). And wow, have these icons left obsessive, anxious, and often irrational marks on your guy's subconscious. Self-loathing, obligation, disappointment, hypochondria, pressure, resentment, duty, and suffering complexes all stem from N&G. Although I'm sure your guy doesn't experience all of the above, I'll bet variations on a theme are his specialty. Unlike a lot of intricate personalities you know, your sweetie won't keep his issues between him, his therapist, and a comfy leather

couch. Jewish men wear conflict on their sleeves. Which means you, my strong Shiksa, have to deal too.

Fret not! Because you were raised to value confidence and aplomb above fear and melodrama, you'll see through his defense mechanisms and not enable or chastise them. Chances are, you'll both learn to laugh at his bundle of nerves. For the sake of your sanity and the relationship's future, start by reminding yourself that his N&G is a cultural artifact, not a sign of weakness. And since it's not in his nature to bottle feelings, your lovable lunatic won't hesitate to talk about them. Shutting him up will be the problem.

And Now, a Word from Our Therapist

According to Carl Weinburg, a prominent New York–
based psychotherapist, Jewish men's psyches are weaned
on two equally strong and opposing views: (1) You're
God's gift to the world; and (2) If you keep your mouth
shut, you won't get into trouble. Consequently, N&G
springs from the question of whether your guy will fit
in—with families, friends, peers, et cetera. If your man
feels his acceptance threatened, Dr. Weinburg says he'll
defend against it with arrogance: He'll either gloat about
successes or, more commonly, become a passive-aggressive
humorist. Jewish men also like to intellectualize, so he
may exhaust you with endless talking and thinking.
When you say, "I feel [blank]," he'll respond, "I think
[blank]." Oh, tomato/tomato. What's important is that
unlike your gentile exes, your Jewish guy's upbringing
was inquisitive and verbal; if compromise is in good sense,
you won't agree for hours about who's right and
wrong—but about what's fair. N&G isn't about control.
"Jewish men are less invested in being right all the time,"
Dr. Weinburg notes. "They prefer self-analysis, which
works to your benefit."

Don't ever doubt your minx appeal or internalize
your guy's blues when he feels underappreciated and

insists no good deed goes unpunished. Instead, let your naturally soothing and nurturing girly assets loose on his fragile tuchus. Whether he's pissed at his boss or sick with sniffles, a Jewish man likes to feel loved, coddled, and respected; he seldom likes to sulk alone. Just so everyone's clear: Dr. Weinburg defines neurosis as "unclear thinking manifested in bad habits," and guilt as "the fear that nothing one does is ever good enough." If the two combine, self-fulfilling prophecy or self-sabotage isn't unheard of. Who has time for that? Take the powerful high road: Be honest about what you fear, understand, and have learned from past experiences. "Men really need guidance in a lot of areas, but it's hard for them to accept it," our savvy Jewish shrink confirms. "Women need to assume the role of leader in a gentle way that lets the man think he's leading." I am Shiksa . . . hear me roar—with laughter, that is.

What's So Funny About N&G?

Not much, from where you sit. But considering comic shtick—from burlesque to the Borscht Belt—grew from Jewish cultural roots, Dr. Weinburg says a good laugh is one of the best and most familiar ways to rescue your man from a phobia or unfounded disappointment without scary confrontation (boo!). "Humor is the language Jewish men speak," says Dr. Weinburg. "If you meet your boyfriend head on, he'll come back head on. Instead, make fun of him. It's like verbal jujitsu: using a person's movement and weight to their disadvantage. Grab on to his words, and twist them around; use them back on him." When dating a Jew, teasing him is the best form of verbal seduction—in more ways than one. Andy, a half-Jewish television producer from Poughkeepsie, New York, says his agnostic girlfriend kills worrywart tendencies by mocking his fears to their extreme. "I'm in constant fear that something bad will happen, whether it's that a chef will overcook my steak or that I'll be mugged on the street," Andy explains. "Dangers are around every corner, and I never stop thinking about a hundred and ninety-two ways to beat them." The more his girlfriend rolls with his rant, the more quickly she diffuses it. "She gets into the spirit of my neurosis, adds to the scenario by hyperbolizing my fears to the nth degree. That's when I become aware of how ridiculous the situation is, and I'm no longer embarrassed to share the crazy thoughts that swim in my head with her."

Although you might think Andy's a new breed of wimp, others (especially Andy) argue he's honing a skill set proven to move execs up the corporate ladder.

"Personally, I see neurotic in-depth planning as a strength," he says. Gabe, a NYC law student, supports his N&G brother: "Neurotics don't make great warriors on the battlefield, but we do make quality professionals. And that's what matters in this world, right now." Or at least on special, expensive occasions like your birthday or the Barneys Warehouse Sale. Listen, I know it's hard to relate to a guy who freaks about minutiae when *your* anxiety, insecurity, and fears stem from big-picture issues such as the impending extinction of the white rhino or how long *Friends* will stay in syndication. But this is yet another reason the Shiksa/Jew connection is so strong: You provide balance to his psyche, and he provides talking points in your relationship. See, everyone wins.

What's in It for You?

Just about anything can make your emotional Weeble Wobble's N&G kick in: from whether your eyebrows are overly waxed to whether you've adequately fawned over his new Paul Smith shirt. Most guys face commitment fears, but in a Jewish man's relationship N&G tends to focus more on specific compatibility details. Quoting an unfamiliar literary reference could make him feel just as insecure about your future as debating whether you both want children. Because his antenna is always up, neurotic ramblings bring make-or-break issues to the forefront that might otherwise be overlooked or buried. "A neurotic person is much quicker to dismiss a relationship because he's spent so much time thinking about their differences," says Gabe. "You kill any phoniness by talking about real issues that much faster. If I weren't neurotic, I'd be shielding myself from seeing the truth about a person or situation."

Hypothesizing about recurring fears, finding comfort in worst-case scenarios . . . it's all a bit exhausting, eh? But hang in, because all relationships should support such honest emotional disclosure. Because you're a stabilizing personality, you won't both think and feel confusion all the time. Howard, a marketing director from Oradell, New Jersey, adds that two highly neurotic attitudes do not a healthy relationship make. "The perfect balance is a woman who analyzes, but doesn't put it all on the table right away and keeps my conscience in check." Learn what buttons cause which reactions (a night with your ex freaks him out because he feels threatened; one with your girlfriends gives him a platform to perform). "The goal in all relationships is to be able to talk about everything, all the time," says Dr. Weinburg. "The more verbal people are, the healthier they are. Feelings have to process into words before they're processed into action." Howard says the average time it takes him to dwell on an N&G thought and reveal it to his partner is a day of thinking and one night of lost sleep. You've had food poisoning that's lasted longer; you can mosey with this.

And It Goes a Little Something Like This

It's one thing to recognize N&G on paper. But to help you spot an N&G personality *when you meet one,* I've excerpted a fully wrought, complex, haughty, tangent-driven monologue from a real N&G subject—and then annotated his obsessive thoughts for further study. Naturally, he will remain nameless to avoid perpetuating excess worry.

"Neurotics are clearly more intellectual and introspective,[1] but neurosis has the potential to cause problems in a relationship.[2] Purely on its own, though, it's harmless—I think.[3] God, it's not like you have ADD, manic-depression, or you're super bipolar. You think about things; you think about them a lot. These things are amplified with caffeine, alcohol, or drug use, of course.[4] But relationships that involve heightened personality types yield neuroses.[5] Now that I think about it, you can also be neurotic about stuff in concert with obsessive-compulsive tendencies,[6] and the next thing you know, you're analyzing it,[7] and you can't stop doing it,[8] and you're completely overwhelmed by it—turning one subject around in your head for weeks or even months on end.[9] Whether you look at it from an emotional side or a romantic side or a physical side, neuroses can be too much sometimes but it's nothing a functioning person can't deal with, I mean . . ."[10]

1. Arrogance, in this case used to legitimize the neurosis caused by explaining neuroses

2. Self-analysis as a means to self-awareness

3. Self-analysis as a means to indecision about self-awareness

4. Sounds like a party to me

5. This is where you come in: love, respect, tease, control, and communicate. Remember?

6. Here we go . . .

7. Yep

8. Nope

9. Welcome, hyperbole.

10. Is Dr. Weinburg still in the house?

Does This Make Catholicism a Guilty Pleasure?

Sure, Catholics believe you'll burn in blistering fires for living in sin or skipping mass to hit Nordstrom's biannual sale. But the guilt Catholics shoulder is very different from what your Jewish boyfriend knows, so don't pretend to understand his N&G just because you forgot to visit the confession booth this week. Leah, a half-Jewish, half-Catholic translator for the Justice Department from Marblehead, Massachusetts, knows both well: "Catholic guilt's taught by the Church to put the fear of God in you. The consequence is eternity in hell. Jewish guilt's taught by Jewish mothers to put the fear of Mom into you. The consequence is worse than hell."

He Said/She Said: Battle of the (Neurotic) Sexes

Let the kvetching begin! Learn how your early dating hang-ups compare to his romantic fixations.

Your Anxious Inner Voice:	His Anxious Inner Voice:
"So how Jewish are we talkin'?"	"So how goyish are we talkin'?"
"Do I look thin in this outfit or is it a skinny mirror?"	"I'll bet she paid retail for that outfit."
"I wonder if he knows my exes. . . ."	"I wonder what she's heard about my exes. . . ."
"Am I as pretty as his exes?"	"Am I as good in bed as her exes?"
"Are those buckles on his shoes?"	"Will she wear that crucifix all the time?"
"Is he gay or just close to his mom?"	"If I keep talking about my shrink, will she think I'm nuts?"
"Should I order a plain salad or steak frites with extra béarnaise?"	"I wonder if she eats kishke?"
"Is that his mother calling . . . again?"	"Is that my ex calling . . . again?"
"Will Mom like me?"	"My family's going to freak about this one."
"Is this guy cute, or am I wasted?"	"She is really hot . . . or maybe I'm just drunk?"
"Does he have premature *ear* hair?"	"Is she staring at my bald spot?"

Your Anxious Inner Voice:	His Anxious Inner Voice:
"Should I pay half or just pretend to reach for my wallet?"	"If she pays half, do we still get to have sex?"
"Did I match my bra and underwear?"	"I wonder if she's wearing underwear. . . ."
"When was the last time he washed these sheets?"	"Is it weird to have sex on sheets my mother gave me?"
"Should I fake it?"	"She's really enjoying this. Crap, she must be faking it."
"How does my first name sound with his last?"	"Does she think sex means we're dating?"
"Wait, was that a friend date or a real date?"	"Oy, she thinks we're dating."
"When will he call?"	"Now I have to call her?"
"If he doesn't, can I e-mail, text, IM, or page him first?"	"Maybe I'll just e-mail after Shabbat."
"Am I destined to die alone with twelve cats and an air fern?"	"Am I destined to live with my family forever?"

CHAPTER 5

The First Shtup

Maybe it's how the moonlight shines on your boy-friend's freckled cheeks, or the way his big green eyes lock with yours after trading inside jokes. You wonder how his exfoliated skin will feel against your naked belly—and that's when your hormones decide to give in to chemistry and curiosity. Tonight's the night.

Before christening your guy's six-hundred-thread-count sheets, mentally brace yourself for a passionate per-formance by a man whose heritage insists his primary goal is to please his lover. Since his attention will always work to your libido's benefit, wondering whether your pleasure is a means to his end should never be an issue. Not when shar-ing an open, sexual experience together is a mutual priority. But there *are* a few things to consider when feeling frisky. . . .

Follow these bedroom crib notes to one sexy shtup.

Stereotypes, Schmereotypes: The Saucy Shiksa

Throughout Jewish history, Shiksas have borne the brunt of an undoubtedly seductive and unfairly whorish reputation. The drama! We're thought to be sirens and gold diggers, femme fatales who use our aggressive wiles to capture the hearts and wallets of Jewish men—and deliberately weaken their family line and sexual resolve. In fact, our insidiously carnal, promiscuous, immoral and insensitive instincts are said to be notoriously and undeniably irresistible.

To that I say: *Meow.*

Flattered? Insulted? Be aware of the above, but please don't take it personally. Here's why: Though playing the role of a bad, bad Shiksa makes for kinky bedtime banter, the truth is that most young, educated Jewish men who date outside their faith don't believe the saucy stereotype to be a modern reality. (It's actually your boyfriend's parents and grandparents you have to worry about. They're the most fearful that the Jewish race will vanish from the earth—and that wanton goyim lead the way.) What your boyfriend and his contemporaries do welcome, however, is everything your unique look, life, and social perspectives introduce to his world—which inevitably includes his bedroom. Ryan, a political activist from Philadelphia, couldn't agree more.

"The fun for me is the clashing of the two worlds," he says. "For example, I would never ask a woman to take off her cross or St. Christopher pendant when we're together. I wouldn't want her to lose her self in the fear of difference." Sandor Gardos, PhD, a Jewish sex therapist and CEO of the San Francisco–based Web site www.MyPleasure.com, insists that it's the loss of novelty that kills passion. "If you're both raised on the same kibbutz and share all the same values, it could get old," he says, adding in half-jest: "Plus, if a man's in bed with another Jew who makes the same nasal sounds his Mom or cousins make, it's not that sexy. A relationship may last longer and your sex life stay hotter if you're from different cultural, religious, and racial backgrounds." Keith, a clinical researcher from Philadelphia who exclusively dates gentiles, is on that bandwagon. "Most of the Jewish girls I've known have similar values, desires, and humor. Dating an unpredictable Shiksa increases mystery, a quality all men find attractive in women."

Get Down and . . . Dirty?

Silently thank his mom—you know, the woman whose sponge might as well be attached to her hand—for her son's obsession with cleanliness and personal hygiene. Just as he'll always squeeze in a shower before a date, he'd never think to sleep next to you without first scrubbing his face and brushing his teeth. So if you expect any action, mimic your man's behavior with Clearasil pads and stolen restaurant mints. I know first-time sleepovers without makeup aren't your usual beauty treatment. But if having a squeaky clean exterior is a trade-off for not worrying about his smelly feet or morning breath, why complain? He'll probably have more products than you, anyway. If ever there were a time to sample Kiehl's Abyssine Eye Cream, this is it.

You already know Jewish men are storytellers. And though your guy will compliment, ask direction, and verbally fantasize in bed (eventually)—do *not* expect him to talk dirty. Dramatic conversation and funny pillow talk break the ice, but please keep it clean. Pay too much attention to his rear, and you'll soil the moment by setting off his yuck alarm. "If a girl puts her fingers near my bum, all I can think is that at some point, they're going to come back near my face, and that's nasty," says Joel, a catering manager from New York. For these reasons, Joel adds that germy anal sex is out, too. "If I ever did this, I'd want to shower immediately. It's just unsanitary." Dr. Gardos says there's method to Josh's madness. "It's safe to assume that Jewish men have a lower threshold for the disgust reaction—an icky response to menstruation and swallowing, for example. This likely goes back to the importance of avoiding the unclean, according to biblical Jewish law." Whether it comes to eating pork or getting porked, most Jewish boys keep it kosher.

Is That a Dreidel in Your Pocket?

We all know size matters, and it's important to communicate this to your Jewish boyfriend. Here's the thing: Your guy, from watching too much stand-up during family trips in the Catskills, may be convinced his penis is smaller than average ("Why do Jewish women like bargains? Because they're used to getting it 20 percent off!" *Ba dum bum*). So when your pookie unleashes his manhood for the first time, bolster his ego or lighten the mood with an obvious compliment about his robust schlong. Personally, my Shiksa friends and I have never met a Jewish man with a small package, unless it's tied with a bow from Fortunoff. In fact, I've always thought Jewish men were exceptionally large. Here's a clinical reality check: "Jewish men *do* tend to be well-endowed, but they're also shorter than the average male," explains

Dr. Gardos. "So it's not that their penises are huge; it's that they're attached to slighter builds, so they look really big." Oh well. Remember that Jewish men are not raised to be macho, so your honey may continue to speak self-deprecatingly about his unit even after you've confirmed otherwise. Consider it a win-win for your libido, because he'll ambitiously work that much harder to make you happy. Jewish men excel as generous, attentive, sensitive, and passionate partners—and for that, you'll be one smiling Shiksa.

Other naked truths: Be sure to feign delight the first time you notice your boyfriend has more body hair than a yak—especially on his pecs, back, and neck. Don't worry. It won't be long before you'll love touching its wiry texture and resting your head on his chest pillow while watching the NBA play-offs (until he puts *you* on Drano duty). One of the most playful, flirty experiences I've ever shared with a Jewish friend was shaving the back of his neck with a triple-blade razor and too much shaving cream. Unfairly, Jewish men's hair issues don't mean they're any more forgiving if *you* forget to shave or wax. Although every Jew secretly wishes he could depilate, he'll insist there's room for only one hairy person in his bed—and that's him.

Finally, you can safely assume your boyfriend won't be covered in tattoos, since he can't be buried in a Jewish cemetery with body art. Then again, if pierced and painted bad boys were your type, you wouldn't be dating someone who answers his mom's phone calls during sex.

It's All About You, Bubeleh—Sort Of

Your boyfriend appreciates that your differences bring a sense of novelty to your rapport, so show him the same about your nookie. The Jewish faith is more open about sex than most religions, so your man will be pleasantly surprised to learn you're willing to abandon inhibitions. Be forward, but also let him initiate new experiences. As one Jewish ex used to remind me, missionary position is an awfully Christian concept. Premarital sex isn't a sin for your boyfriend, because he doesn't believe in hell.

A Jewish man will literally bend over backward (or upside down or from behind . . .) to please a woman. Again, thank his matriarchal culture for this. (Like it or not, Mom will always be in bed with you. Jewish men spend their lives gaining her approval; I suspect your guy's interest in making you moan is a twisted extension of this.) If he needs to move a little to the left to hit your sweet spot, guide him. As Colby, a writer from Manhattan, insists: "Jewish men, by nature, rely on their wisdom and guile. We love to be taught, so tell us what you want. We always want to rise to the top, which includes learning good sex skills." Lucky for you, your guy's eager-to-please MO includes an admitted obsession with giving oral sex— so resist naming your cutesy vagina after things he can't eat, such as shellfish or pork. Above all, don't forget to twist, scream, and giggle with gratitude. Not sure you'll orgasm? For the love of Abraham, fake it so he doesn't develop yet another guilt complex.

Just realize that in the throes of passion, using the Lord's name in vain could be confusing: "Oh Jesus, I am coming . . ." might sound like you're dying, not climaxing.

According to Dr. Gardos, you'll benefit from making your love machine feel in control of his prowess. "A gentile woman who doesn't hyper-analyze their encounter will make her man a better lover, guaranteed. Jewish men are always more attentive, which pleases women—but Jewish men also get off on their ability to make a woman happy," he says. "It's a good vicious cycle." Even Colby confirms that *giving* lovers aren't always *selfless* lovers. "*I* want to feel good about making a woman come, so it's not exactly altruism," laughs Colby. "Sex isn't UNICEF, for Christ's sake." Reassure your boyfriend that you like how he kisses your neck or touches your hips to shortcut post-game analysis. "The key to good sex is not being cerebral, and Jewish men have trouble with this," says Dr. Gardos. One last point: Because your guy overreacts and exaggerates by nature, the last thing you want is for him to tell you (and believe himself) that he's gay or has erection issues because you forgot to host a ticker tape parade in his honor. Think about it. The first party ever thrown for him—the bris—celebrated his penis. Which might just say it all.

"Did You Hear About . . . ?"

Regina, a photographer and budding Buddhist raised in Germany, describes her early sex life with her Jewish husband, Alex, a New York creative director, as tender, intimate, and germ-fearing. Allergies are no stranger to Regina's immune system—and soon after the couple became intimate, they made a cameo in Alex's boudoir.

"One of the first times Alex and I made love, I got a bloody nose from my allergies. I think it was ragweed season," she explains. Rather than freak out, Alex calmly brought Regina tissues; the bleeding stopped, and the two continued to have sex. When Regina bled a second time, more intensely, the couple switched positions: Alex held an ice pack to Regina's nose. Only after a *third* run did the flow stop. "It was so embarrassing!" Regina laughs. "But Alex was really cool about it. He just took care of the problem—and of me."

Alex's fluffy feather bed didn't help Regina's allergies either. To offset their sinusitis sex, Alex surprised Regina with new pillows, sheets, and a comforter. "He bought the most beautiful hypoallergenic bedding for his room so I wouldn't feel stuffy when I stayed over. It was so thoughtful." Although Regina dated men from many cultural and religious backgrounds before meeting Alex, she insists that he, like most Jewish men she's known, is especially warm and considerate in the bedroom (especially when circumventing sickness). According to Regina: "The fact that Alex redecorated just to make me feel better is one of the more unique ways he's proved to be protective, caring, and nurturing in bed." One can only imagine how similarly attentive Alex is *between* their sanitized sheets. . . .

If Ever a Jew Knew: Q&A with Sean

My friend Sean, dubbed a "Super Jew" by *Time Out New York* and a "Power-Pop Mensch" by *The Village Voice,* runs the irreverent songwriter series "What I Like About Jew" (www.seanaltman.com). More important, he's one randy Jewish lover who's enjoyed his welcome in Shiksa social circles. In his prime, Sean claims to have bedded a gaggle of gentiles—one of whom he was married to briefly. And yes, Sean's naughty lyrics support his open-minded rep. In a song titled "Jews for Jesus," he croons: "I've disobeyed the code of Abraham / I've eaten several Shiksas and some ham."

No wonder I asked Sean to answer questions from amorous Shiksas, anxious for info about shtupping their Jewish men. He's like Dear Abby . . . but with more body hair (and, well, a penis).

Q: I've been dating my first Jewish boyfriend, David, for a few weeks, but we haven't slept together yet. What should I expect? —Charlotte, Delaware

A: Expect to be pleasantly surprised. Jewish men have been weaned to believe they'll inevitably be persecuted. So they will, like Avis, try harder. This translates into more enthusiastic foreplay, endless cunnilingus, and even (yes, way!) afterplay. But don't expect David to have an athletic body when you see him naked. Your boyfriend will never be a jock; at most he'll just be an athletic Jew. We love sports, but we're better at watching and spouting stats than playing. Pumping iron is considered goyish, if not gayish. The wise Shiksa appreciates her Jewboy's love handles (or pretends to). One of my songs goes: "If you can't handle my love handles, then you can't handle my love."

Q: I'm a big fan of pillow talk. What sweet nothings should I whisper in my Jewish boyfriend's ear?
—Caroline, Nebraska

A: Say something nice about the size/shape of his penis. Better yet: Sing it! Shout it! Praise him in rhyme! Here's a nothing *not* to whisper: "Yasser Arafat had soulful eyes." Don't discuss Middle East politics, as few people of any political persuasion agree on this topic. It's a no-win discussion. You'll likely say something he perceives as anti-Semitic, and he'll lose the mighty erection you've nursed to perfection.

Q: I grew up in Europe, so I'm used to uncircumcised penises. In the States, I've been with Jewish men— but I never want to touch their penises, because they look so different! Will they feel different too? —Gabrielle, Minnesota

A: Not once it's inside you, unless he mistakenly wears his yarmulke on the wrong head. Don't be surprised if you like his American bald eagle better. Who needs the extra skin? And cheese-smelling smegma? To the Europeans' credit, the foreskin on an uncircumcised penis supposedly makes sex more pleasurable for the man. I've experimented by pleasuring myself with a cold cut (kosher, of course). The difference was negligible, and I ruined a perfectly good slice of corned beef.

Q: For a Jewish guy, what's the worst thing that could happen while having sex with a Shiksa? —Carey Ann, Tennessee

A: Either she'd only agree to perform oral sex if I did her taxes, or her cross would lacerate my thigh while she's performing oral sex. Or both.

"Did You Hear About . . . ?"

I was casually dating the cutest LA transplant named Max for a few months, when he asked if we could spend Yom Kippur together. Rather than suggest we attend temple and fast till hypoglycemia set in, the novelist proposed an art flick and lunch at our favorite French restaurant. From what I could tell, Max was comfortable with tweaking the rules of religious convention . . . until we had sex that night. After an impressive go, Max began to cry. Did our intimate encounter move Max to tears? I wish! Turns out, my guy bawled because he felt crippled with guilt for making whoopee on Yom Kippur.

That's right, ladies. Devout Jews don't knock boots on the Day of Atonement (more on this later). Who knew? Christians have sex on Christ's birthday all the time; and even on Easter, our most sacred holiday, I can't think of any God-fearing gentiles who'd turn down a healthy romp. Talk about playing the role of a Shiksa stereotype. Short of donning a crucifix and yelling "Holy mother of God!" when I orgasmed, I felt like the reckless woman who lured her man into his bed and out of his religious habits. After Max's tearful confession, I apologized profusely, kissed him on the forehead, and bolted from his apartment before I could hear him pray for forgiveness. The Day of Atonement may end at sundown, but don't ask your Jewish man to rise until the morning after.

CHAPTER 6

Why Antacids Are the Fifth Food Group

Whether you're eating bagels and lox with your boyfriend or making dinner for his fussy family, food and its significance in the Jewish home are heavy issues. And by heavy, I mean both loaded with meaning and incredibly rich and caloric. When you date a Jewish man, you commit to (1) spending more time with your personal trainer, (2) stocking your medicine chest with antacids, and (3) savoring every snack and meal—or else dodging family whispers about your potential eating disorder(s). Also expect to chow more than three times a day *and* snack after 8 p.m. I bet you feel bloated just thinking about it.

Food is the center of all Jewish social interaction, which means you'll reach your man's heart by showing his stomach some love. If your boyfriend were to redefine the FDA food pyramid, he'd create food groups from brisket, kugel, dill pickles, blintzes, chicken soup, potato latkes, chopped liver, rugalach, lox, gefilte fish, and kosher franks. Dietary fiber, vitamins, and minerals are for pills taken after his a.m. bialy.

This is why I've gathered fun, fixable Jewish recipes for your hungry man in this chapter—and answered the age-old question: "What is kosher, anyway?" Shopping and dieting tips for JFCs (Jewish Food Converts) are also included. I've ignored the history of pickles or what to order from a deli menu. If your little knish has a special request or interest not discussed in this chapter, call a caterer.

Pork: The Diseased White Meat

Kosher laws are a very detailed, complex body of Jewish dietary regulations, so we'll stick to the 101 version. Ahem: Kosher comes from the Hebrew word "kasher," which translates to approved, fit, and permitted. To be kosher, mammals must have split hooves and chew their cud, while birds must fly—though lazier fowl like chicken and turkey are okay. Fish must have scales and fins, which means shellfish is out (sorry, shrimp cocktail lovers!). So are crawling animals, no matter how gourmet, like escargot. Dairy and meat can't be served or consumed at the same time, which means ham and cheese sandwiches do not a romantic picnic make. (Plus, he'll need six hours between milk and meat dishes to digest. That's a lot of small talk.) Fruits, veggies, grains, eggs, and fish are neutral foods. Kosher laws also include rules for separate kitchens, dishes, silverware, pots, and pans—but your boyfriend, even if he was raised to keep kosher, probably won't expect your grandmother's Lenox to be properly arranged and sterile (especially since they're not dishwasher safe). In fact, he's probably a vegetarian to simplify things. If keeping kosher is very important to your sweetheart, make it easy on yourself and appoint him designated chef.

In general, kosher is about being clean—and this includes food eaten, which then purifies the soul. While Moses was busy parting the Red Sea and carving the Ten Commandments, fellow Israelites dropped like flies from diseases caused by unsanitary conditions and spoiled foods (kosher delights are still dried or salted to preserve). The laws were also created to instill communal self-discipline, limit the number of animals one can kill and eat, and cause revulsion at bloodshed—among other dictates. Separating meat from milk comes from the biblical warning not to boil a calf in its mother's milk; Jewish principles also insist on separating life from death: Milk signifies life, and meat symbolizes death.

Even if your boyfriend doesn't keep kosher, he may still avoid pigs in the form of honey-glazed hams, chops, ribs, or roasts because he's been weaned on thinking the oinkers carry disease. (Note: Most Jews say really crispy bacon doesn't count. Don't ask me why. . . .) A few years ago I promised a Mexican fiesta to my Jewish friend Sam and his new roommate Paul—and coined myself a culinary whiz when www.epicurious.com's "Mexican-Style Cheese and Sausage Casserole" bubbled over with Monterey Jack and meaty goodness. Although Sam helped himself to seconds, Paul pushed his food around his plate and filled up on margaritas. Only three years later did I learn that Paul's family kept kosher—and nobody told me. The lesson? When playing hostess, it's your responsibility to ask.

Rub the Buddha

We know your man loves to eat. If you're eating out, he'll inspect, analyze, and ask about meals at neighboring tables—God forbid he make a poor choice—yet still switch plates with you halfway through a meal (rather than slice a corner of his chicken for your bread plate). Just as your honey devours you in bed, he'll similarly attack all things delicious or within arm's reach. He'll be disappointed and concerned about your eating habits if you don't do the same. Ironically, Jewish men share a universal "fat guy" complex, which likely stems from a food-pushing mama or mean playground jokes. Combat your lover's fears by complimenting his developed chest or strong arms . . . but never his abs. He'll see through you like cheap lingerie.

Once your boyfriend's tummy is full, rub it in circular motions, pepper it with kisses, then tell him to gulp Maalox, Pepto-Bismol, or Milk of Magnesia. Sympathize with his complaints, hypothesize about its cause, and ask if he's up for Chinese tomorrow night. Although you, in such a gut-busting state, might force yourself to only eat grapefruits for a week . . . Jewish men suffer from gastronomic amnesia. His credo: Another day, another chance to feel heartburn.

Fish-n-Tips from Russ & Daughters

Russ & Daughters, located in NYC's Lower East Side, is world famous for its caviar, smoked fish, and specialty foods (www.russanddaughters.com). Since 1914 the store's been run by four generations of the Russ family—most recently, Joshua Russ Tupper, the family's fourth generation and the store's heir apparent.

According to Josh, smoked fish is "Jewish soul food" and will remind your boyfriend of his youth. To tug at his heartstrings, Josh suggests a massive brunch for multifaith friends with strong stomachs. This includes smoked salmon, sable (cold smoked black cod with paprika), whitefish, whitefish salad, cream cheese (chives or plain), pickled herring, and bagels—with rugalach and babka for dessert. A few shopping tips from the expert:

1. When choosing whitefish, go fatty for maximum flavor and moistness.

2. Buy larger filets of pickled herring, and if you feel adventurous, slice the fish with a cream and pickled onion sauce for a creamed herring spread.

3. Demand thinly sliced salmon. No fish, especially salmon, should ever smell like it came from the Hudson River.

4. Buy from a store in which you can trust the advice of the counter staff—and don't be afraid to ask questions. Taste away! If you don't sample, how will you know if the salmon is nicely salted or the sable acceptably moist?

Make Him Come Back for More

So what if the only recipes in your repertoire are lasagna and slice-and-bake cookies? Remember that your boyfriend is predisposed to appreciate food for how it nourishes his body and relationships, so even if you blow a new culinary attempt, he'll eat it to avoid hurting your feelings. Use these homespun Jewish recipes to feed your boyfriend's heart—and if these rations don't do the trick, make reservations.

Nana's Chicken Soup

Serve with cooked tender egg noodles or matzo balls.

Eric, a publicist from Atlantic City, New Jersey, called his nana while suffering from a cold. Although Eric's live-in girlfriend at the time, Claudia—an Italian Catholic from Brooklyn—provided her sweetie with enough Tylenol, tissues, and flat ginger ale to keep him comfortable . . . Eric's nana thought she could do better.

"Neither Eric nor I cook, to the point where we get bills from our electric company asking why we don't use gas in our apartment," Claudia says. "So when Eric's nana began listing ingredients for her chicken soup over the phone, assuming I'd whip it up, I wanted to put her at ease." Claudia's solution was a recipe for disaster. "I told Nana I ordered Eric chicken soup from a great Cuban spot down the street that delivers," Claudia remembers. "She wasn't impressed." According to Nana, this is what Claudia should have made. . . .

1 large fryer chicken. Buy chicken parts already quartered.

6 or more peeled and quartered medium to large yellow onions. Need enough to fill the

bottom of a 6- to 7-quart pot with a lid. If the onions are large, cut into more than quarters, but not thin slices.

1 whole celery. Clean and cut stalks in 3- to 4-inch lengths. Chop white, dirty ends. Remove thin, leafy tops and save to place on top of the cooking soup.

1 11-pound bag of carrots. Clean and cut into same size pieces as celery stalks.

Salt and coarse pepper to taste.

Cover bottom of pot with onions. Lay chicken parts skin side up over onions, as flat as possible. Lay thin, leafy celery tops on top of chicken. Add cold water—just enough to cover chicken and bring to full boil—then reduce to a simmer and cover. Cook for about 2 hours. Stir gently and taste for flavor, while adding salt and pepper to taste. For a rich savor, let soup cook a bit longer. Add cut carrots and celery to pot, and continue to simmer with lid for 15–30 more minutes.

Test vegetables: They should be tender, but not soft. Gently remove chicken parts with slotted spoon or tongs, and place in separate bowl. Carefully transfer carrots and celery to separate bowl. Chicken can be separated from bones when cooled. The tender, flavorful pieces can be added to the bowl when serving soup in small portions. They also make for a great chicken salad.

Chill soup broth in refrigerator. Skim fat off top of soup and discard. (Fat will congeal on cold soup, which makes it easier to remove.)

To reheat: Simmer soup over low flame. Carrots and celery can be reheated in small amount of soup in a separate pot, and then added to soup when serving.

Terry's Potato Latkes and Applesauce

Terry, a lapsed Catholic from Media, Pennsylvania, prides herself on the first Jewish recipe she ever learned—and hasn't stopped making for twenty years. According to this Shiksa mom, "I make a nice potato pancake with homemade applesauce and sour cream. The problem is that I always want to serve it with pork roast." Her recipe was adopted from a cookbook she bought at Temple Israel of White Plains when her daughter Lina attended preschool there. Terry learned about how to make fast and authentic Jewish dishes with her food processor that have impressed her interfaith family time and again. This is her first and favorite.

For latkes:

4 medium Idaho/russet potatoes, about 2
    pounds, peeled, cut to fit food processor
1 medium onion, about 6 ounces
2 large eggs, lightly beaten
1/3 cup flour
1 teaspoon baking powder
3/4 teaspoon salt
Freshly ground pepper
Oil for frying (canola or vegetable)

Grate potatoes in food processor using very light pressure, then empty potatoes into colander. Rinse under cold water to remove starch. Add to large bowl and cover with cold water until ready to use. Grate onion in food processor. Drain potatoes and squeeze out liquid (wrap in towel to really squeeze dry). Add onions and other ingredients to potatoes, and mix well. Fill large skillet with 1/8 inch of oil. When hot, shape potato mixture into patties (about 1/3 cup of mixture) and place into pan on spatula to avoid splattering. Brown well on both sides. Drain on paper towels.

To reheat: Preheat oven to 450 degrees. Place pancakes in single layer on ungreased, foil-lined cookie sheet. Bake uncovered for 7 to 8 minutes, until crisp and hot.

For applesauce:

One apple per person
Water

Core apples and cut in quarters. Cook in pot with about 1/4 cup water on medium heat until they're soft. Add apples to a food mill to get rid of skins. Finished applesauce will be pink from skins. Refrigerate until ready to eat.

For sour cream:

"Nobody makes their own sour cream." —Terry

Amy's Reuben

Finger sandwiches are for old bats and baby showers. Amy, a Jewish fashion designer from Ocean, New Jersey, makes overstuffed Reubens when she invites her boyfriend's friends over for their notorious pool parties. "Men don't have to be Jewish to love a good New York Reuben," she says. "They have to love to eat."

8 slices of pumpernickel or rye bread
1/2 pound of thinly sliced corned beef
1 cup drained sauerkraut

2 to 3 tablespoons of Thousand Island dressing
4 slices of Swiss cheese
2 tablespoons of butter

Pile corned beef, sauerkraut, salad dressing, and cheese on four slices of bread. Top with other bread slices. Spread margarine on outsides of each sandwich. Grill on griddle, skillet, or under broiler until bread browns and cheese melts.

Bella's Kosher Strudel

"Making my strudel is a very long process. Two hours! But it's also a very special thing," says Bella, my friends' granny living in Encino, California. Although Bella was born in Poland, she moved to Germany when she was sixteen and immigrated to the United States in 1952. Bella learned this strudel recipe from *her* mom—and has made it for Rosh Hashanah for thirty-five years (she saves it for the holiday because it's so laborious). Because Bella memorized her recipe, I've approximated ingredient amounts below (there's a lot of sprinkling here). Expect to have more filling than necessary so you can add, improvise, or subtract to taste. "You don't measure these things," she insists. "You have to feel it to make it. If your strudel's not right the first time? Practice."

Set aside:

1 cup of flour
1 egg
Oil
Vinegar
Water (room temperature)
2 large McIntosh apples
1 bag of raisins
1 bag of sliced almonds
4 tablespoons of cinnamon
1 pound of sugar
1 pound of bread crumbs
1 jar of strawberry or raspberry preserves

Dough:

Sift one cup of flour with pinch of salt into large bowl. Punch indentation in middle, and add one egg, a tablespoon of sugar, a teaspoon of oil, and a teaspoon of vinegar. Add 4 ounces of water and stir with a fork (or until the mixture begins to absorb and stick). You will not use all flour. Roll dough on plastic cutting board. Knead with fingers, as you would bread. Add more flour until you form a little ball of dough. Put dough back into bowl, and cover with plate to keep at room temperature.

Filling:

Peel and shred two large apples. Line up all ingredients, each in small pudding cups: cinnamon, raisins, almonds, sugar, and preserves. Sprinkle clean dish towel with flour. Oil cookie sheet so strudel won't stick.

Split dough ball in half and knead a second time. Roll out one piece with rolling pin until paper thin, always sprinkling with flour so it doesn't stick. Dip knuckles in flour, place hands under dough, and stretch dough with knuckles in every direction. Patch together if it tears. Place this on flour cloth, stretching it in every direction to make it thin and large. Repeat process with second dough ball.

Sprinkle both dough sheets with oil from pastry brush. *Always* leave an inch around its edge empty and dry for sealing later. With first sheet, sprinkle bread crumbs over dough (not too thick—it will absorb moisture). Divide grated apples in half, then spread apples and cinnamon on dough. Add more bread crumbs over the apples, and sprinkle with more oil, a tablespoon of sugar, raisins, almonds, and preserves—according to preference. Lift one end of cloth and roll it like a jellyroll, while sealing ends of pastry. Place on cookie sheet so end of strudel is on bottom of cookie sheet and top is solid dough. Repeat process with second dough sheet.

When both rolls are on same cookie sheet, brush both with oil. Preheat oven to 375 degrees, then bake for an hour until brown. Slice while hot, let slices cool, then serve.

Seth's Chocolate Bagel Pudding

When I dated Seth, a civil engineer from Portland, I wanted to make a dish reminiscent of our recent Caribbean vacay—but spice things up with extra cayenne pepper rub. After we burned our mouths with blackened meat, Seth debuted a sweet family recipe to relax our palates. Bad move by me, nice save by Seth. Enter: Chocolate Bagel Pudding.

4 cups of half-and-half
4 cups milk
6 eggs
2 yolks
1/2 teaspoon ground cinnamon
2 tablespoons vanilla extract
3/4 pound dark break-up chocolate

1 8-ounce container of sugar
Bagel cubes of 1/2 inches with the crust
  removed

Whisk eggs, sugar, cinnamon, and vanilla together in bowl until very smooth. Add milk and heavy cream. Place bagel pieces in two medium-size trays and add mix. Let mixture sit for 1 hour, stirring occasionally to be sure that bagels get wet. Pour half of mixture from one tray in a medium-size white baking dish, and add chocolate cut in pieces and other half of mixture. Sprinkle top with some small pieces of chocolate. Put baking dish in big tray with one inch of hot of water and bake for an hour at 300 degrees.

When It's More Than a Schmear

So your slender frame isn't made for two-slice minimums of cheesecake? Bonnie Taub-Dix, a Jewish certified dietician with the American Dietetic Association, suggests these tips for keeping your goyish—I mean, girlish—figure. Hey, at least you don't have to skimp on mayonnaise.

1. Scoop out the doughy part of your bagel for low-fat cream cheese or egg whites.

2. Know your breads. Light rye, marble rye, and pumpernickel are easiest to digest and high in fiber. Challah is made from eggs, eggs, and more eggs—and is torn off in chunks, rather than sliced. This means one piece of challah can equal three ounces of bread!

3. If given a choice, go fish. It's low in saturated fat, calories, and cholesterol.

4. If your guy keeps kosher, margarine is his friend. But it's no amigo of your hips! Margarine has the same calories as butter and contains trans fats, so think twice before spreading this artificial substitute on your bagel.

5. You know better than to say you won't eat Bubbe's hamantaschen because you've sworn off sweets for bathing suit season. The alternative: "I'm stuffed, but this looks so good I'd love to take some home with me!"

CHAPTER 7

Talk Yiddish to Me

In any new relationship, you've got to talk the talk. And in this case, honey, you're talking Yiddish. Yiddish, which literally means "Jewish," is a derivative of German dialect that's mixed with Hebrew and Slavic languages—and was once nearly exclusive to Jews in and from Eastern and Central Europe. These days, Yiddish is more likely to be overheard in the game room of a Palm Springs retirement home than in the hip coffee shop where you chill with your hunk—though all Jews (American-born, too) do sprinkle their speech with this dialect. In fact, more common Yiddish words like "schmooze" or "glitch" have been incorporated into English.

Though your guy prefers you don't bastardize his ancestors' dialect with a southern drawl or deep-throated WASP intonations, you'd be meshuganah not to memorize

key phrases of his occasional vocab. Plus, the closer you two get, the more time you'll spend with his family—and you know what that means. Even when you're still in the room, everyone will have an opinion about you. Do you honestly think his grandmother whispers in English?

The last thing your boyfriend wants is for you to pretend you're Jewish, but you can expect bits of Yiddish to fly from your pursed lips at any given moment; these words are spoken so emphatically that they're more contagious than poison ivy. Chances are, you've spouted Yiddish terms before and never realized their etymology. Remember when that schmuck cut you off on Route 70 without a signal? I rest my case.

You Too Can Speak a Second Language

The trick to learning Yiddish, as with any language, is to listen up—especially since sounding-out written words won't help as most are written phonetically and inconsistently spelled. Note where your boyfriend places accents and when his sister makes phlegm-like choking noises. Some say Yiddish is a dying language among young generations, but I don't buy it. Most Jews I know include Yiddish in their daily vocab without even thinking about it. That said, be careful: Mispronouncing words or using them at the wrong time can also make you sound ignorant. Nobody wants that.

Of course, the other extreme is to force Yiddish into chitchats and sound like a poseur. Remember how annoying it was when Madonna began speaking with a British accent after dating Guy Ritchie and moving to London? Don't make the same bloody mistake. Also, once you know

Yiddish basics, you'll be tempted to upgrade with coordinating shoulder shrugs and hand gestures. Resist! Words like schmutz and farklempt lend themselves to physical posturing, but waving your hand or scrunching your eyebrows for effect will remind everyone of Aunt Sylvia when she plays yenta. And we all know how hot that is.

Regardless, I say throw your guy a colorful stinger every once in a while to show you're paying attention. Yiddish is a funny language from a storytelling heritage, but some of its best phrases aren't used very often. If your boyfriend's own people aren't going to keep the good ones in circulation, who's he to stop *you* from trying? For example, the next time you're in the mood for Italian but he fights for sushi, tell him: "Gey kaken afn yam." ("Go crap in the river.") Or if he expects praise for emptying the dishwasher, even though he left the utensil basket full, tell him: "It will helfen wiie toiten bunkis." ("That's as helpful as trying to wake a dead person.")

Yiddish Terms to Wow Your Man and Confuse Your Spell Check

Take a deep breath, Shiksa darlings. I've put together a list of today's most frequently used Yiddish terms—ideal for family eavesdropping, personal memorization, or spicy pillow talk. If you're confused about pronunciation, ask Jewish friends or the local JCC for help. Vocal nuances vary and Webster's breakdowns are no good here. Come on, does Webster sound like a Jewish name to you?

alter kakher:	An old fart
bashert:	Fated
bopkis:	Of little value
bubele:	Term of endearment, like "honey" or "sweetie"
chutzpah:	Guts, nerve
dreck:	Junk
farklempt:	Choked-up
farshtunken:	A stinky situation
feygele:	A male homosexual
frum:	A religious person
glitch:	A slipup
goy:	Refers to anyone who isn't Jewish, but literally means "stranger"
klutz:	Bumbling person
knaker:	A big shot
kosher:	Beyond its food meaning, "kosher" also refers to all things clean and legit
kvetch:	A complainer

L'chaim!:	A Jewish toast, "To Life!"
maven:	An expert
mazel tov:	Congratulations
mensch:	A good man
meshuganah:	Crazy
mezuzah:	An encased scroll affixed to the right side of the door-post at a Jewish home as a reminder of God's presence
mishpocheh:	Family
mitzvah:	A good deed
nebbish:	A frumpy man
nosh:	A snack; a "nosher" is one who snacks a lot
Nu?:	So? Well?
ongepotchket:	Refers to a woman's tacky outfit, usually thrown together in a mishmash
Oy gevald!:	Oh no!
plotz:	To explode with emotion
punam:	Face; "shayna punam" means beautiful face
pupik:	Belly button
putz:	An incapable person who often screws up; literally also means penis

schlemiel:	A foolish, clumsy person
schlep:	To drag
schlock:	A lazy person or sloppy item
schmaltzy:	Overly sentimental to the point of nausea (or at least ridicule)
schmattah:	Rag, dress
schmoozing:	Chatting
schmuck:	A male jerk, or more literally, a penis
schmutz:	Dirt, or to muddy a situation
schnapps:	Booze
schnorrer:	A gold digger
schnoz:	A big nose
schpeel:	To go on and on and on . . . about a topic
shadchen:	Matchmaker, who makes shiddachs (matches)
shande:	A disgrace or shame
shaygetz:	A non-Jewish male
shiddach:	A match, made by a matchmaker
Shiksa:	A non-Jewish woman
shlemazel:	A born loser
shlumpy:	Like "frumpy," used to describe someone who's a slob or a mess

shpilkes:	Nervousness, being too anxious to sit still
shpritz:	Spray
shtick:	A comedy routine for which a person is known
shvitz:	To sweat
traif:	Not kosher
tsimmes:	A fuss; the word is derived from a stew that *simmers*. Get it?
tsuris:	Troubles or misfortune
tuchus:	Your bum
tzetummelt:	Mixed up
yenta:	A gossipy woman

"Did You Hear About . . . ?"

In the mid-1920s, my immigrant grandparents moved to the Italian enclave of Newark, New Jersey—which was miles away from the city's Jewish neighborhood. But because my grandfather was a tailor and it was his job to talk schmattah with Jewish garmentos, he brought home scraps of the Yiddish language. He flavored broken

English with Jewish terms, as if it were fresh cream in a traditional Bolognese. I swear on my grandfather's Singer that it wasn't until I dated my first Jewish boyfriend in college that I realized the words "schmooze," "putz," and "schlock" weren't slang from the Old Country.

The Only Word You *Really* Need to Know

Chutzpah. This gritty noun celebrates guts, nerve, balls— but only in the very best way. It's a word that defies propriety, while applauding those who act without reservation and with complete audacity. Chutzpah is your "Get out of Bitch Jail Free" card for antagonistic actions, feisty thoughts, or unedited words that might otherwise be considered, well, a tad obnoxious. And all this time, you've been blaming your alter ego on PMS.

Consider: You snatch the last Marc Jacobs tote at Loehmann's, well aware that another shopper saw it first. You're not a selfish, aggressive brat. You have *chutzpah*.

Consider: You spy a beautiful, bejeweled woman coupled with a wrinkly old hobbit and throw her a knowing smirk that says, "He must have one hell of an insurance plan." You're not a nervy, nosey snot. You have *chutzpah*.

Consider: Your underpaid assistant spends three sleepless nights writing a proposal for which you take full credit in a company-wide meeting. You're not a thoughtless, opportunistic bitch ... oh wait. In this case, you definitely are.

Yiddish Mad Libs: A Love Letter

Who doesn't pine for a love letter from a secret admirer, made all the more dreamy by lyrical Yiddish cadences? Use your new vocab to fill in the blanks of this note, written by a Jewish man to his unrequited Shiksa interest. Simply replace the English definitions with Yiddish terms. Isn't it romantic?

My Dearest _____,
                (Term of Endearment)
I don't want to sound _____, but when I saw
                      (overly mushy)
your long, blond hair blowing in the Vineyard breeze
last week, your _____ veiled only by your crisp
                 (belly button)
linen _____, I felt myself _____. I was
      (dress)   (sweat profusely)
_____—even more than the time I spied you
(choked-up)
in a Black Dog T-shirt . . . and nothing else. But as I
drew closer, I noticed some _____ on your
                            (dirt)
_____—and though I wanted to brush it off, I
(bum)
was afraid of acting like a _____. So I _____
                           (jerk)   (sprayed)
your _____ with my water bottle instead,
     (bum)
though you likely suspected an ocean mist. Alas, I know
I'm a _____, but sometimes my family
      (born loser)
wonders if I'm just a _____. Either way, my
                     (male homosexual)
love for your _____ is true. Maybe someday I'll
             (beautiful face)
have the _____ to say "hello" or even "nice
        (nerve)
_____." Until we meet again, when I'm an
(belly button)
_____ with a _____ habit . . .
(old fart)   (booze)
Yours in _____,
        (misfortune)
Seth

CHAPTER 8

The Jewish Mother

Yes, your boyfriend's mother gets her own chapter. She wouldn't have it any other way! Ingratiate yourself with her immediately, or confront the face of endless scrutiny and meddling for the rest of your relationship. Believe me, it's a face that only a Jewish son could love.

His mother is not only the familial gatekeeper but also the center of all emotional bonds. She's one hell of an Alpha Mom, with primal instincts that push her to (1) protect her son at all costs and (2) insist he can do no wrong. And you know what this means: Your relationship with him is, and always will be, intrinsically tied to her relationship with you. Really, it's not as painful as it sounds. In fact, you can use it to your advantage.

So what's a Shiksa to do when she meets her boyfriend's mom?

Be Her

Your mom always said that being yourself wins hearts. But what does *she* know? Your mom's not Jewish, and although applying this adage may impress your man, it probably won't have the same effect on his mother. Because cloning isn't an option, most Jewish moms want to know that the *other* women in their sons' lives are just like them (give or take a few pounds). In an ideal world, you two would smell alike, dress alike, cook alike, hug alike, shop alike, talk alike, and laugh alike . . . regardless of whether you're a temp or full-time family fixture. Worried about whether your parallel role will make his mom secretly feel threatened? Silly Shiksa, unspoken intimidation is for WASPs! A Jewish mom will be impressed that you two have so much in common. Don't be disingenuous; just be . . . strategic. Examine Mom and her home, visibly gushing over both, the minute you walk through the door. Memorize visual clues that point to similar interests, and immediately translate them into feverish chitchat. Peppering your interactions with his mom's habits, behavior, and dialogue will help everyone digest their brisket that much more easily.

Take Good Care of Her Boy

Your boyfriend's mom has worked very hard to mold him into the cutest little Oedipus complex you've ever met. Could you show some appreciation? Make peace with the fact that you will always be the second most important woman in his life—then affectionately demonstrate how much you care about your boyfriend to score major points with the woman who gave him life. Just ask Dianne, a Jewish mother of two boys from Wisconsin who share an (admittedly cliché) obsession with Catholic girls. "Jewish moms are very physical with their sons, so I need to see a Shiksa hug and touch my baby to prove her affection," she says. "I want to know that she nurtures him like I do." When Mom's watching, reach for his arm or move his hair from his face to say you're subtly doting. Worrying, dwelling, suffering, begrudging, or becoming frustrated by something you can't control—on behalf of your boyfriend—shows her you care. Don't forget to feign hypochondria on her son's behalf! Remind her of how proud, happy, and safe he makes you feel—and how thankful you are that she raised such an (insert blush-worthy adjective here) young man. When you're alone with your boyfriend, use Mom's MO to prove you're terribly shrewd. Occasionally mimic her moves—a hand on the shoulder, a kiss on the forehead—to subconsciously put your sweetheart at ease when coaxing him out of a downward mood swing or into a Tiffany shopping spree.

Chew the Fat—and Her Food

Get ready for brutal honesty on her part, and serious self-divulging on yours. "When girls meet my mom, she expects them to divulge immediately," says Josh, a copy-writer from Canton, Massachusetts, who's dated his share of blond-haired, blue-eyed Swedes. "She'll poke and prod, but she'll also disclose. Judaism is all about openness. Any non-Jew I bring home has to get ready to get personal." Always follow Mom's conversational lead, but know that it's an open forum for perceptive assessments (not to be confused with criticism) and clever storytelling (not to be mistaken for exaggerated fibs). Go on, gripe about your nasty boss or laugh at your sister's wretched taste in men. Outside of refusing second helpings at dinner, few words will shock Mom's ears. But don't be surprised when she's terribly blunt with you, too. "My youngest son dates a Scottish girl," explains Cindy, a Jewish mom from Boston. "Every time she visits, I make her pesto, muffins, cookies . . . and when I went to her house for the first time? Nothing. She served me water. You'd think she'd buy a little coffee or juice or milk or muffins for her boyfriend's mom." If *you* think Cindy kept her opinions from the Scottish lass, then someone hasn't been paying attention. Although a Jewish mom may seem deliberately brash or curiously revealing at first, her criticisms are harmless because she knows no other way. Even better, she can dish it *and* take it: a rare maternal combo that will work to your advantage down the road. Embrace her honesty, and appreciate that

Mom's candid openness simply means she wants what's best for her family—and that includes strong communication about everyone's feelings. If those aren't signs of acceptance and love, I don't know what are.

"Did You Hear About . . . ?"

My friend Julie, an Episcopalian graphic designer from Manhattan, dated a Jewish man named Greg for almost a year before he introduced her to his mom; basically, he hoped to guard his Shiksa from Mom's analysis as long as possible. Just before the two women met, Greg gave Julie a pep talk. "Mom's very protective and has always taken a minute to warm up to my non-Jewish girlfriends," he explained. "So don't take her inquisition too personally. Eventually, she'll love you!" Julie nervously asked if there was anything else she should know about Greg's mom before their encounter. "Well, she also left my father for an Israeli lesbian pilot," he said, coolly. "Her girlfriend will be at dinner too." Julie exploded with laughter: "Are you kidding me? Your mom's liberal enough to date a woman who flies into combat areas for a living, but she's going to judge me for being a Christian?" Enough said.

Don't Speak the Mother Tongue?
So You'll Learn

To an untrained ear, a Jewish mom seems to speak her own language. But once you learn to interpret her lexicon, you'll soon realize that what appears to be gross hyperbole or passive-aggressive understatement is nothing more than a tête-à-tête. Not allowed to finish a sentence? This means she's actually interested in what you're saying. Jewish mothers love enthusiastic repartee, so don't fight the following:

1. To build a relationship with your guy's mom, keep in touch regularly. Phone calls, thank-you notes, or small gifts that reflect shared encounters or inside jokes are expected—I mean, always appreciated.

If She Says:

"Sylvia's son's girlfriend calls *her* once a week."

She Really Means:

"So how do you plan to top that?"

How to React:

Call and send cards to say you're thinking of her on special occasions. These include Mom's birthday, anniversary, and weekly canasta games.

2. Jewish mothers speak in dramatic extremes, with facial expressions and hand gestures that make wrinkle creams and quick reflexes a must. Have you ever known something mediocre to happen to a Jewish mom? Whether she's opening a gift or a jar of pickles,

the event is either fabulous or horrifying. Even mundane feelings are cause for emphatic self-expression: She's completely exhausted, but never tired; starving to death, but never hungry; absolutely freezing, but never cold. Correcting her won't put her at ease; agreeing and empathizing with her concerns will.

If She Says:

"I'm freezing to death under this air conditioner. I should've brought a sweater."

She Really Means:

"If I get sick and miss my Kabbalah class, you'll never hear the end of it."

How to React:

Ask the waiter if you can change seats (far from air ducts *and* kitchen help). Offer your blazer to drape over her shoulders.

3. To a Jewish mom, food is love and demonstrative of a giving soul. The only thing worse than forgetting to announce that her kugel is the best she's ever made (*every* time she makes it) at her table . . . is serving her cold, processed, or frozen edibles when she's in your home.

If She Says:

"Bagels and lox? Really, you shouldn't have."

She Really Means:

"Thawed Lenders and vacuum-sealed salmon? You *really* shouldn't have."

How to React:

Ask where she buys her smoked fish, and hit the fresh bagel shop before visits. Knowing Mom's favorite pastries, and memorizing the bakery's delivery number, can be a lifesaver too.

4. Jewish moms don't take no for an answer very easily. They're a cunning lot, who aren't afraid to use their domestic clout to provoke action through guilt and persistence. Tonight, do what she asks. Don't be taken aback by martyrdom and long faces—especially when tolerance earns bonus points with your man. Just keep in mind that this is *not* an example of how mimicking Mom's behavior will deepen your relationship with her son. Chances are, your guy finds your nudge-free persona novel and attractive. A man who's dating a Shiksa is not a man who wants two moms.

If She Says:

"What do you mean, you don't eat boiled chicken? Here, taste this."

She Really Means:

"I slaved over this meal for five hours, and it's my specialty. Try some. You could stand to put some meat on your bones."

How to React:

Clean your plate.

5. Pay attention to all complaints of physical ailments. Whether Mom's suffering from a runny nose or waiting to hear test results from her specialist, she'll appreciate the audience. Act as if her grievances impress you, and tell her that your aunt Martha endured a similar illness (but never one that's more agonizing than hers). Compare each problem's rarity and how many opinions it may take before reaching a diagnosis. Suggest a temporary solution.

If She Says:

"My sciatica is killing me."

"My back hurts. Get me an ice pack."

Insist that you make her an appointment with your neurologist, the best in town. He's always booked solid and outrageously expensive, but definitely worth the money.

"Did You Hear About . . . ?"

"I always feel like a walking target at Noah's house," says Marie, an Irish Catholic Internet marketing exec from Rhode Island—and the only Shiksa girlfriend ever to be introduced to Mom (Noah's two brothers only date Jewish women). Marie met her thirty-one-year-old guy's mom for the first time at a birthday dinner and immediately noticed how openly lenient she was with her sons. "No conversation was off limits," Marie remembers. "Sex, drugs, criminal records. The brothers turned buried secrets into funny anecdotes, while Mom just laughed right along. She has an underlying allowance and faith in her sons that took some getting used to. My family is so proper and judgmental. We couldn't be more different."

Now Marie has a great relationship with her darling's mom—but preps ahead for each encounter with self-deprecating jokes or amusing stories. "I'm so clearly not Jewish that the only way I can fit in is to vehemently admit that I'm so Irish and Catholic. We all poke fun at how foreign their nuances are to me. I've built quite a backbone."

Dote, Gloat, and Emote (Like Stop, Drop, and Roll . . . Only Your Nervous System's on Fire)

If you and Mom have run out of sales to compare, problems to analyze, and neighbors to gossip about . . . don't panic! Default to emergency action: "Dote, Gloat, and Emote"—about her son, that is. A Jewish mom loves to hear about her son's generosity, success, and brilliance since she connects so much of her own self-worth to his achievements. When you Dote, Gloat, and Emote, she'll feel secure that you adore her son and all she's done for him (even when she's not around to remind you).

Here's how: Ardently connect your boyfriend's past achievements to his current character, all of which indirectly praise her. Realize that your shtick will provide a springboard for maternal boasting, which (1) buys time until you initiate the next topic and (2) tells you which turns down memory lane are most important to the family. Speak with an offhand tone and ask rhetorical questions so she doesn't think you're kissing up. Soon, you'll have more than enough storytelling ammo for family banter *and* private talk with your beau.

Carol, the Jewish mother of a good boy from Boca Raton, suggests the following Dote, Gloat, and Emote scenarios and tips. For the sake of this exercise, let's say you're dating a guy named Adam (believe me, if you date enough Jews, eventually this will happen).

Scenario:

Adam played baseball as a kid, and now he coaches Little League.

Dote:

"You should see how sweet Adam is to his right fielders. So encouraging and attentive . . ."

Gloat:

"I was so proud of him when his team won the championships. All those years you spent schlepping him to Little League are paying off."

Emote:

Touch your own heart—just for a second—while singing your guy's coaching praises.

●●●

Scenario:

Ask to see a family album, complete with naked potty pictures and Adam's first Hava Nagila. Gush over any physical trait that mirrors Mom's DNA.

Dote:

"Look at that little toosh! And those big green eyes! They must be inherited from your side of the family— the gorgeous eyes, I mean."

Gloat:

Tell her how just last week a stranger mistook her son for Noah Wyle—you know, the sexy Jewish bleeding heart from *ER*.

Emote:

Later, rub his knee and watch his eyes light up when you retell the Noah story: "So cute. He hasn't changed a bit since he was a baby!"

Scenario:

Adam picks up the dinner check at a posh restaurant—for you and his family.

Dote:

"He's always so generous. It's so nice to be with a gentleman. . . ."

Gloat:

"How rare to date someone with good taste *and* good manners. You raised such a prince."

Emote:

Wink knowingly in Mom's direction.

• •

Scenario:

You're making coffee and small talk with Adam's mother.

Dote:

"I love watching Adam play with his nephew. Is it true that Jewish men make the best husbands?"

Gloat:

Brag about how impressed you were when Adam, at a

recent business dinner, credited family as the silent supporters of success.

"I don't know how you raised a family, started your own business—and still made it to step aerobics five days a week. I hope to do it all someday too. . . ."

"Did You Hear About . . . ?"

Like all Jewish mothers, Sheryl from Chicago wanted her son to be happy in his new relationship—and accepted his Korean-American girlfriend, Kyung, with open arms. Early on, Sheryl adamantly shared her version of a dating must with Kyung. "I told her that when you first start dating, you must set a precedent with men right away and tell them how it's going to be," says Sheryl. Kyung was a quick study. Early in the couple's relationship, Sheryl recalls having dinner at Kyung's house. At one point, her son asked his girlfriend to please pour his father a drink. According to Mom: "Kyung told him, 'If he wants a drink, then get up and get it for him.' Later I told her, 'Good girl. You did just as you should.'"

Today the couple is happily married with two sons—and Kyung, who was previously a born-again Christian, has converted to Judaism. Which makes Kyung a Jewish mother herself . . . with a very astute teacher.

CHAPTER 9

Mishpocheh and the Hanukkah Bush

Once you're in Mom's good graces, winning over the rest of the gang is a piece of cake (preferably macaroon). Simply recognize the family hierarchy and then nuzzle your way into their hearts according to each person's interests and priorities. In this chapter, I've lumped together family gatherings with holiday basics, because you'll likely do most meet-n-greets at Passover dinner or before services at the local synagogue.

Brace yourself for a loud, affectionate, inquisitive, animated, and food-focused welcome! With any family gathering, first impressions matter. And when your lovebug introduces his best Shiksa? They *really* matter. Arrive fully manicured, wearing a look that reveals minimal cleavage; lose the uptight Lilly Pulitzer prints or anything with the Lacoste alligator. Never show up empty-handed: Fresh flowers, such as tulips or irises, or Jewish sweet treats are dear gestures. During the holidays, choose a nice kosher wine over the typical Manishevitz—and stay away from generic gifts like Godiva chocolates or French soaps. You already know that Jews love food, so play to their appetites. "My parents are always impressed when Shiksa girlfriends give expensive salts, imported jams, or fancy bottles of vinegar they'll never open," says Zach, a thirty-year-old attorney from Pleasantville, New York. "These food gifts show you're in the financial position to buy something totally useless but can still appreciate its highbrow significance."

Abandon personal boundaries the second you spy his family's mezuzah, because your life is now the conversation du jour. His loved ones aren't familiar with your history, so it's your job to put anxieties, humor, and family relationships on the table—without turning the event into a dear diary excerpt. "Usually when I meet new people and want to acclimate to an unfamiliar situation, I'd sit quietly and ask a lot of questions to show interest," says Mandy, a twenty-seven-year-old Catholic restaurateur from Sun Valley, Idaho. "But that's a wrong move when you meet a Jewish family.

The more silent you are, the more suspicious they become. The second you out your neuroses, the family's familiar with your antics and comfortable with your personality."

Don't worry, girls. It's a fair swap. You'll know his relatives' emphatic feelings about everything from gay marriage to Uncle Ivan's angina ten minutes into appetizers (not that you asked). Even now that they're engaged, Barbara, a Catholic editor from upstate New York, still finds the home life of her fiancé, David, a screenwriter from Long Island, to be a bit jarring. "My family's emotions are buried under ten layers of rock," Barbara says. "Meeting David's family, especially his mom, who can't stop talking about how much she likes me, was overwhelming at first. My own mom doesn't compliment me half as much! I also knew how everyone felt, every second of the day. Sometimes I can't believe David's family will be mine for the rest of my life."

Whether you hang out for life or just until dessert ends, family ingratiation is a big deal. Here's what to expect from each member, according to how important their influence is in the overall Jewish family unit.

1. Mom and Your Boyfriend:

You already know how to win Mom's heart, and since you're dating her son, we'll skip this part. Male siblings come next, but they're just happy to have someone new to banter with. Moving on . . .

2. His Sisters:

Bond just as you would with a new girlfriend. Talk boys, pedicures, frozen yogurt, and scooped-out bagels. Suggest an insider salon that's mastered the eyebrow wax. Don't tell them you have lots of JAP friends in an effort to connect. Share endearing stories about their brother, because, like moms, sisters want to know he's loved—and that you're not some floozy slut.

3. His Dad:

Unlike most gentile families, Jewish dads are the weakest links in the hierarchy. Mom rules the roost, so Dad secretly wishes he were more masculine than he's allowed to be. He's probably pressured your guy into playing basketball and fixing carburetors simply because he can't. Clue in to Dad's insecurities, laugh at his jokes and stories, and assure him that his son's an accomplished figure—especially in the boardroom, since drive and success are important to Jewish fathers. Assure Dad you're not interested in his son's money, that you're a one-man woman. If he's a fat cat, ask questions that demonstrate intellectual curiosity, and talk about international travel or favorite books (except maybe this one). Dad may live vicariously through his son, in which case he's happy about you as the decorous gentile; as I've said, there's a torn and unspoken premium on a Shiksa's nature among older generations. It's also very important to reveal an astute and clever personality. Whatever value it carries for Dad's son to be with a hot Shiksa, it's more humiliating to know he's with a stupid one.

4. His Grandparents:

Your sugar's grandparents, often called Bubbe and Zadie, will be the hardest personalities to penetrate. Because interfaith dating was a complete abhorrence when they were young, the fact that their grandson fell for someone who's not a member of the tribe may seem—sorry, ladies—a disgrace. In fact, Jews traditionally declared their children dead if they married gentiles. You'll have to work overtime to convince this pair that you're worthy of their affection (try even harder if he's the first-born son). If she likes you, Bubbe will squeeze and prod in uncomfortable spots and mention something about eating you up—even if she's had three helpings of brisket. This is a good thing. Slip it in that you visited your own grandparents last week so they know you're family oriented, or take the couple out for pistachio ice cream and share your touching Rosh Hashanah resolutions. Don't leave too early, or they'll assume you're bored with conversation. Eventually you'll win his grandparents' hearts too.

Okay? Okay. Now that you've met the family, you'll feel at home during Jewish holidays. Before you run off to shul, keep a few things in mind: (1) Jewish holidays honor religious events about human beings, unlike Christian holidays that double up with imaginary characters for nonpious gluttons (Easter celebrates Christ's resurrection *and* mall bunnies that lay chocolate eggs); (2) Jewish holidays are broken into festivals, holidays, and fast days—so know when to be solemn and when to rejoice; (3) Jewish holidays are not an excuse to get wasted on Manishevitz. Unless your boyfriend is with his buddies, most Jews—at least as a family—drink very little, and so should you; (4) If you should forget everything you're about to learn, wish his relatives a heartfelt "Gut Yontif!" ("Happy Holiday!") and know he owes you big time when *your* major celebrations roll around.

Back to Shul: Rosh Hashanah and Yom Kippur

Rosh Hashanah and Yom Kippur are considered High Holy Days (Rosh Hashanah translates to "head of the year" in Hebrew, while Yom Kippur means "Day of Atonement"). The two holidays have ten days of penitence squeezed in between, during which your sinful boyfriend repents for his transgressions and devises means for self-improvement. Since these are the most important holidays of the year, you'll want to spend them together—which means buying or booking synagogue tickets in advance. Temple accommodations are more coveted than nosebleed seats at a Fleetwood Mac reunion.

During Rosh Hashanah service, don't jump when

a congregation member blows the shofar—aka a ram's horn. Although Rosh Hashanah celebrates the Jewish New Year, the shofar is in no way related to the toys and noisemakers you're familiar with blowing on December 31. Rather, Jews believe the sound of the shofar reaches God's ears and reminds him to open the Book of Life, a catalog of Jewish names that separate good souls from bad.

On Yom Kippur, your boyfriend fasts from sundown until sunset the next day. Too weak and hungry to do much else, he'll pray for forgiveness of sins that include fraud, arrogance, hypocrisy, gossip, sexual immorality, and maybe even dating you. Not only will he abstain from eating and drinking, but also he'll stay away from sex, bathing, wearing leather, and anointing the body with oils. I suggest you book a spa treatment when he's not looking, because your body is as good as useless to him. After a day of fasting, your sweetly suffering martyr will gorge himself at a Break the Fast feast. How pleasant to be physically reunited as he stuffs his face with whitefish. For the truly devoted, fasting with your guy will bring you closer. And just think: Your stomach will be much flatter from not eating once your sex life resumes!

When to Observe:

Early fall (September/October)

What to Wear:

Impressive dress or suit; leather skirts, pants, belts, purses, and shoes are fashion no-no's.

What to Bring:

Basket or cornucopia of apples and a pot of honey; gum and hard candies for Break the Fast breath

What to Drink:

Sip, don't swig, the wine. If you fast together, you'll feel lightheaded from not eating.

What to Say:

"Shannah Tovah!" impresses the family, but "Happy New Year!" works too.

The Big Do:

Wear comfy shoes to temple, and take naps to kill fasting time. Before the holiday, practice eating and assembling unfamiliar foods so you'll nosh like a pro at Break the Fast.

The Bigger Don't:

Ask if you can borrow your man's silk or wool tallis to kill a draft. This white, fringed shawl is worn for prayer during morning services and Yom Kippur.

Back to Shul: Passover

During Passover, Jewish families celebrate the Exodus from Egypt and freedom for Jews everywhere (remember Charlton Heston in *The Ten Commandments*?). Their real cross to bear is that they also nibble matzo, a type of unleavened bread, for eight days. This is the dry, bland cracker that Israelites ate when escaping from the Egyptians, because they couldn't wait for bread to rise. A series of rituals during the seder dinner occurs in a very specific sequence to tell the Exodus story, formally called the Haggadah. Everyone at the table, including you, will read from the script during dinner.

All food on the seder plate symbolizes events in the story. Ask your boyfriend to explain their meaning to you before dinner, so you can focus on not puking from the sight of shank bone, green vegetables, roasted or hard-boiled eggs, bitter herbs, and charoset (a mixture of apples, nuts, wine, and cinnamon) on the resistible seder spread. Don't question your host's thrifty ways when the middle matzo, or afikoman, mysteriously disappears from the stack—and children are sent wildly searching for it later. Instead, encourage the curious tots, because once they find the missing cracker, dinner is over. Although a seder meal isn't exactly five-star dining, the best part is you'll be encouraged to drink four cups of kosher wine to wash it down. This is not the time to ask for a nice Shiraz instead.

One last thing: The youngest person at the table will read the Four Questions, a series of q's that highlight the seder story's importance. Let's hope your man has young relatives and isn't robbing the cradle with you—otherwise, guess who's solo in the spotlight with gefilte fish stuck between her teeth?

When to Observe:

Eight days in March or April

What to Wear:

Your Easter finest, including whites

What to Bring:

Kosher Pesach desserts made without yeast, kosher wine, flowers

What to Drink:

Manishevitz, but not the extra glass in the middle of the table. It's for Elijah, who never shows up (so rude), but that doesn't mean it's fair game if you need a social lubricant.

What to Say:

Your parts during the Haggadah, like it or not. "Love that matzo!" sounds sincere, too.

The Big Do:

Download a Passover script from the Internet for practice; making the gentile talk during the seder doubles as Jewish dinner theater. You'll have monologues, so repeating "watermelon, watermelon" like you do during church prayers won't cut it.

The Bigger Don't:

Whine, "Are we finished yet?" as the Haggadah goes on and on. This reading can take anywhere from twenty minutes to four hours. Suck a lozenge. Good luck.

Back to Shul: Hanukkah

Hanukkah, the Festival of Lights, celebrates the defeat of Antiochus Epiphanes, the Seleucid king of Syria who tried to force the Greek religion on Jews by occupying their Holy Temple. He filled it with idols and sacrificed pigs, redefined laws and denied Jewish rituals. Consequently a man named Judah Maccabee led a war against Epiphanes—and won! Yet when the Jewish soldiers reclaimed the temple, they found enough oil to light their lamps for only one day. But as miracles go, the oil burned for eight.

In this story, oil represents freedom—and also gives your man's family reason to eat jelly donuts and potato pancakes, fried in oil, to celebrate the big victory. In homage, your boyfriend's family also lights a nine-pronged menorah, one day at a time. After a blessing, the candles are left to burn down—nobody ever blows them out (this isn't a birthday party, girls). Lit candles are only used to honor the holiday, never for reading or mood lighting a foyer. Most families place menorahs in windows to spread the good news.

When it comes to gift giving, don't be surprised if your baby and his family hand out modest treats for eight days. Books, CDs, and other small items are the norm. Because we Shiksas are demanding and greedy in December, most interfaith couples I know follow Christmas gifting traditions: stocking stuffers and big gifts! Want to stash presents under a Hanukkah bush? Flip a gelt (gold-coin chocolate) to reach that iffy decision— or better yet, spin the dreidel to win a happy medium.

When to Observe:

Eight days during December

What to Wear:

Casual dress clothes in any colors but red and green

What to Bring:

Artsy Hanukkah candles and gourmet Hanukkah gelt

What to Drink:

Just enough champagne during a Hanukkah party to have fun. Mind your buzz. . . .

What to Say:

"Happy Hanukkah!" to his fam. "You call that a gift?" to your boyfriend, if you unwrap microwave slippers as a present.

The Big Do:

Remain flinch-free when you hear your boyfriend pray in Hebrew for the first time. Don't laugh, even if you are slightly uncomfortable.

The Bigger Don't:

Dress like Santa—or worse, one of his sexy little elves to be cheeky

"Did You Hear About . . . ?"

When Siobhan, an Irish Catholic jewelry designer from Ridgewood, New Jersey, and her Jewish husband, Michael, first met with their wedding coordinator, it wasn't their own needs and priorities that they first addressed—it was their families'. "We realized we were financially screwed because the bar needed to be stacked for my Irish family and we couldn't skimp on food because of his Jewish family," Siobhan laughs. "That's when we thought about our poor future child. We knew if he didn't become a major alcoholic, he'd be a little chunk monster. Or worse yet, both!" Liam Isaac, the couple's infant son, *did* borrow from both cultures . . . but so far, only by name.

Menorah Must-Nots

5. Do not place the menorah under a hanging house-plant.

4. Do not suggest dripping hot candle wax on your body during foreplay.

3. Even if his home reeks of stuffed cabbage, do not replace candles with incense sticks.

2. Be careful striking a match. Uncle Joel's Jew fro is highly flammable.

1. Yes, it's inappropriate to light your cigarette with a menorah.

Dreidel Gambling Tips

4. Don't be afraid to ask for rules. Most Jews forget them when they're ten years old.

3. Suggest playing for real money. Raisins, nuts, and pennies won't pay your December Saks bill.

2. Feeling antisocial? Hide the top under snoozing Uncle Shimmel.

1. Don't suggest a drinking version. Ever.

"Did You Hear About . . . ?"

A Jewish mom from Maryland, Dale has only invited two of her son's girlfriends into her home (both Christian). "I know my son dates a lot, but he only manages to bring home Shiksas," she says. Though both women were on their best behavior during their visits, Dale insists that an ideal meet-the-family night would go something like this:

"My son's Shiksa arrives with a gift she didn't pay retail for and announces that the kitchen smells delicious. She compliments my outfit, while never wearing a cardigan, a belt, or socks embroidered with hunting horns or small ducks. She asks my son if he needs a snack before dinner since they've been traveling all day, just as she begins small talk. She spills details about her life, mentioning any Jews in her family—even if they're seven generations removed. She doesn't waste her breath on brothers employed as cops or marines. At dinner, the Shiksa serves my son his meal and eats every last bite of her own (no picking allowed!). She empathizes with how much I sacrifice for my son, and shares her concern about whether he has the right health insurance and 401(k) plan. Finally, the happy couple thanks me profusely, leaves early . . . and acts like sex is the furthest thing from their minds."

AFTERWORD

Boy Vey! You're Practically Jewish!

Not really. But I do bet that you, my dear Shiksa, probably know more about dating a Jew than your boyfriend does. Mazel tov . . . and then some! At this point, I'll meddle no more. Not because I've exhausted my sage goy wisdom, but because I'm giddy with confidence that you now understand how to properly date members of the tribe *and* be the envy of your same-faith friends. What more do you need to know?

Okay, maybe this: Any further questions you have about your boyfriend's beliefs are probably best answered by Jewish friends, your boyfriend, or his mother. Obviously, the Shiksa/Jew model isn't foolproof. But the way I see it, you two have earned the huge benefit of exploring personal growth and new cultures simply by spending time together. Enjoy! And to think, it all started by wanting to play hide the matzo on more than just Passover . . .

Oh, and in case you were wondering, all subjects in this book are still living happily ever after as enlightened Shiksa singles or loving interfaith couples. I wish I could take credit for their eureka moments and blissful unions. Instead, I'll just take credit for yours.

SOURCES

The following sources helped me provide you with useful info about Jewish culture . . . so you could become the ultimate Shiksa girlfriend. And now you are!

Benvenuto, Christine. *Shiksa: The Gentile Woman in the Jewish World*. New York: St. Martins Press, 2004.

Steingroot, Ira. *All-Purpose Yiddish Knowledge Cards*. Pomegranate Communications Inc.

Weiss, Vikki, and Jennifer A. Block. *What to Do When You're Dating a Jew: Everything You Need to Know from Matzah Balls to Marriage*. New York: Three Rivers Press, 2000.